PRAISE FOR $UCCESS NOW! FOR ARTISTS

"*Success Now!* is a gem of a book and worth its weight in gold for its invaluable information and practical advice for the artist." **Nancy di Benedetto, Art Historian, Author of *History of American Art,* and lecturer, Metropolitan Museum of Art**

"Renée Phillips sounds the clarion call for self-empowerment and is the voice to the artist of the 21st century." **Bernard Olshan, Artist, National Academy Museum and former Vice-President, American Society of American Artists**

"This book has inspired me to make positive changes in my career. If I had read it earlier I would have avoided making many costly mistakes." **Lori Weinless Fischler, Artist and President of the Westside Arts Coalition**

"Renée is all about helping artists become successful. Her book makes the business end more approachable." **Cornelia Seckel, *Art Times***

"Renée Phillips is one of the most informed advocates and motivating members of the art community – both nationally and internationally. In this book, working from a deep spiritual base and focused conviction, she fuses a plethora of information to address the needs and concerns of the artist." **Sandra Indig, Artist and Psychotherapist**

"I have never met anyone in the art world like Renée Phillips who is so singularly focused in her pursuit to help artists establish and further their careers." **Edward Rubin, New York Art Writer, and member of the International Association of Art Critics**

continued

"Renée Phillips inspires, guides and encourages artists to reach their goals through sound advice on the business of art. Her seminars are standing-room-only." **Regina Stewart, Executive Director, New York Artists Equity Association**

"This book is a wake up call for artists to take control of their careers, and not leave them to chance or the vagaries of the marketplace." **Lynne Friedman, Artist and former President of New York Society of Women Artists**

"Your book *Success Now!* gave me the courage to turn my life around. Your message is clear. It changed my attitude towards a number of misconceptions *vis a vis* my art, the art world, as well as my private life." **George E. Homsy, Artist**

"This book is not only full of extremely useful and interesting information, it is also empathetic, encouraging and inspiring. It makes one feel that there is a warm and caring person cheering them. That is relatively unusual and means a lot!" **Andrea de Castano, Artist**

"*Success Now!* has taught me the proactive habits and marketing strategies that I use on a daily basis." **Frank Bruno, Artist and Artist Advisor**

"You inspired me to think larger in terms of getting my art out into the world." **Mira Fink, Artist**

"Your book has been of immeasurable help to in terms of explaining the business of art. Thank you for writing your book with a generosity of spirit, which comes through loud and clear."
Laraine Jablon, Artist

SUCCESS
NOW!
for
ARTISTS

A Motivational Guide
for The Artrepreneur

RENÉE PHILLIPS
The Artrepreneur Coach™

MANHATTAN ARTS
INTERNATIONAL

REVISED AND EXPANDED SECOND EDITION

Success Now! For Artists

Unattributed quotations are by Renée Phillips

Published by Manhattan Arts International
200 East 72 Street, Suite 26L, New York, NY 10021
Tel: 212-472-1660
E-mail: info@ManhattanArts.com
www.ManhattanArts.com

Manhattan Arts International is also the publisher of *The Complete Guide to New York Art Galleries* and *Presentation Power Tools For Fine Artists.*

Success Now! For Artists
Library of Congress Catalog Card Number: 97-75488
ISBN 0-9719881-8-8
First Edition 1999
Second Edition 2003
Second Printing 2004
Third Printing 2005
Fourth Printing with revisions 2006

Cover design by Elijah Blyden/Crunch-Time Graphics
Printed in the United States of America

DEDICATION

In memory of my mother Elyse Green.
Her unconditional love and confidence in me will
forever be a source of inspiration.

ACKNOWLEDGMENTS

This book would not exist without the rewarding relationships I have enjoyed with artists, artists' agents and other professionals for more than twenty years. I thank everyone who encouraged me to write this book and waited patiently for it after the first edition sold out.

The process of creating this book was a joyful team effort. I thank Judy Herczfeld Hoffmannn and Michael Jason for their editorial assistance. A warm appreciation goes to Elijah Blyden, Artist and graphic designer, for this spectacular new cover. My gratitude goes to many friends and colleagues who have endorsed this book and contributed their sage advice, quotes and passages, including (listed alphabetically) Andrew Abrams, agent and business coach, Janet Appel, publicist, Joan Arbeiter, Artist and art educator, Margaret Danielak, owner of DanielakArt, Nancy di Benedetto, art historian and curator, Eleanor Dickinson, Artist and professor, Lori Weinless Fischler, Artist and President of the Westside Arts Coalition, Lynne Friedman, Artist and former President of New York Society of Women Artists, Frances P. Harris, Partner in Blumberg & Harris, Inc., Art Management/Consultants, Sandra Indig, Artist and psychotherapist, Donna Marxer, Artist and artist advocate, Bernard Olshan, Artist, National Academy Museum, Marcelle Harwell Pachnowski, Artist and President of National Association of Women Artists, Edward Rubin, art writer and fellow member of the International Association of Art Critics, Regina Stewart, Artist and Executive Director of New York Artists Equity Association, Cornelia Seckel, Publisher of *Art Times*, Corinne Shane, President of InestinArt, an art advisory firm, Carole Sorrel, Principal of Carole Sorell Incorporated, a public relations firm, E.J. Weiss, Artist and Curator and Melissa Wolf, Executive Director of Women's Studio Center.

My heartfelt thanks go to the loyal subscribers of *Success Now! The Artrepreneur Newsletter*™ and to all of you who have attended my seminars, sought my counsel and purchased *The Complete Guide To New York Art Galleries* and *Presentation Power Tools For Fine Artists.*

This book would not have come to fruition without the support of my immediate family including my brother's Pete's friendship and astute counsel and my Aunt Sharon's spiritual guidance. During the process of writing this book I was comforted by the memories of the dearly departed including my mother Elyse and her unconditional love, my sister Selene and her extraordinary artistic talent, my Aunt Gertie's humanitarianism, my father Zoltan's artistic heritage and my step-father Gordon's mentorship.

My life and work are greatly inspired by the younger generation comprised of my nephews, Michael and Jason, my nieces Cheri and Vanessa, and my cousins Jessica and Michael who lovingly remind me each day that creativity is the perfect child within us. It is a precious gift that must be respected and nurtured, and allowed to blossom fully, because it is the essence of our souls and a path to our enlightenment.

Success
should not
be measured
by external events –
when you sell your first work,
or have your first one-person show,
or get a positive review by a critic,
or when your work is collected by a museum.
It should be a constant flame that glows
steadily and triumphantly within you –
originating from the knowledge
that you create your destiny.
You don't need anyone –
a dealer, an agent, an art critic or patron –
to give you validation or approval.
Success – is yours – Now!

TABLE OF CONTENTS

Introduction

Follow your bliss.

Joseph Campbell

This book is a tribute to the artist who has the impulse to raise their voice and claim their identity. It is a companion to the artist who feels isolated during the solitary process of producing their art. It champions the artist who is passionately devoted to the creative process and who perseveres regardless of the uncontrollable forces that threaten their creative freedom. This book is for artists of all ages, career levels, creative styles and media.

For two decades I have been blessed with having the opportunity to counsel thousands of full- and part-time artists and agents from around the globe working in a wide range of styles and media. Their ages, education and ethnic backgrounds are as diverse as their professions that support their art. I have counseled administrators, educators and advertising executives, one of the Beatles' personal photographers, a Nobel Prize winner, a well-known television actor, and a noted plastic surgeon. Aspiring and established artists have sought my advice on a variety of subjects from creating a business plan, to selecting a gallery, to generating publicity. This book contains many of those experiences and the strategies I have used.

The title of this book is familiar to those who have been reading *Success Now! The Artrepreneur Newsletter*™ since its first issue in 1991. "Success Now!" is also the title of many seminars I have presented in art organizations and institutions such as the American Society of Contemporary Artists, Heckscher Museum, New York Artist's Equity Association and NYC College Art Teachers Association. "The Successful Artist in the New Millennium" was the title of the series of workshops I presented as an adjunct faculty member of Marymount Manhattan College.

My good friend and esteemed art writer Edward Rubin has referred to my writing as "a compendium of compassion and a labor of love." He is familiar with the topics in this book about which I have discussed with great passion in my seminars and private consultations, as well as articles I have written for *Manhattan Arts International* magazine, *Success Now! The Artrepreneur Newsletter*™, *The Artist's Proof, FYI, Chicago Arts Coalition News* and many other publications.

The quotes, in addition to my own, originate from three primary sources: *Artist to Artist*, compiled by Clint Brown; *An Artist's Book of Inspiration*, compiled and edited by Astrid Fitzgerald; and *And I Quote*, by Ashton Applewhite, William R. Evans III and Andrew Frothingham. This quote from Deepak Chopra's book *The Seven Laws of Success* reflects my philosophy and the meaning behind this book:

You are what your deep, driving desire is.

As you desire it, so is your will.

As you will it, so is your deed.

As your deed is, so is your destiny.

Brihadaranyaka Upanishad IV. 4.5

You have to leave the city of your comfort
and go into the wilderness of your intuition.
What you'll discover will be wonderful.
What you'll discover will be yourself.
Alan Alda

WHY I WROTE THIS BOOK

Since I began public speaking two decades ago, I've observed a tremendous growth in the number of creative individuals who are determined to take charge of their careers. To meet this demand I provide career consultations for artists around the world. I answer dozens of calls and e-mails each day, maintain an artist resource web site and e-zine, and I conduct career workshops each month. Artists ask a myriad of questions and share their concerns and dreams with me. I help them steer their career and confirm their goals with advice and informational resources. This book enables me to share many of the career-building tools and techniques I have put to practice in this competitive field.

To my dismay, although graduates of art school enter the real world with artistic techniques and knowledge of art history, they are less equipped to navigate in the world of business. This book gives me the tool to reach out to them and fill that void.

No matter how much talent an artist has he or she will flounder without career goals and guidance. And, no matter how much financial security an artist has if they aren't creatively nourished they will suffer. To be fulfilled an artist needs to acquire balance between creative satisfaction and financial security. This book provides simple and practical solutions to help artists triumph in the areas of creating, marketing, selling and promotion. It provides inspiring essays and many questions to ignite creative solutions and lead artists on their own path to personal and professional satisfaction.

I wrote this book *Success Now! For Artists* as an invitation for you to discover and develop your innate talent, become more courageous and self-sufficient, and pursue your dreams in a place of serenity and celebration. I hope you open this book often and that you will find the inspiration and help you need at many different stages of your professional journey.

Life is
either a daring adventure or nothing.
Helen Keller

The process of writing this book began in 1991 but the meaning of *Success Now!* became more urgent to me in the last few years, in the face of two personal tragedies. One was the loss of my sister, a loving, beautiful and talented woman whose life came to an abrupt end from breast cancer before she could achieve her extraordinary creative potential. The initial process of writing this book during my mourning period was a tremendous healing force for me.

Shortly following my sister's death, my mother was diagnosed with Alzheimer's Disease which took her life on November 8, 2005. With each stage of the disease new challenges in learning to understand and cope tested and developed my capacity for compassion, patience and communication. These experiences have fueled me to become more persistent and passionate as a catalyst and motivator. I have learned that this moment is all we have and that we must make the most of it *Now!*

The September 11th disaster and the events that have since unfolded have shaped a new world in which we realize the importance of cherishing every precious moment. The impetus behind my words is my desire to share, to learn and to grow with you. In the back of the book you will find "80 Mantras for Success", a place you can go to quickly recharge your batteries.

The insightful words of Henry Miller offer reassurance and direction:

Everything we shut our eyes to,
everything we run away from,
everything we deny, denigrate or despise,
serves to defeat us in the end.
What seems nasty, painful, evil, can become a source
of beauty, joy, and strength, if faced with an open mind.
Every moment is a golden one for him
who has the vision to recognize it as such.

SELF-DISCOVERY

From an early age there are people and events that guide us on the path to self-discovery – to reveal our life's purpose. I believe our misfortunes are our best resources to help us transform adversity into strengths. As a painfully shy and sensitive child I found solace and creative expression in classical music, ballet, art and poetry. Growing up financially challenged I learned to be resourceful. As a daughter of an alcoholic, raging father I channeled my feelings of fear and powerlessness into scholastic achievement and student advocacy. My reaction to my father's illness instilled in me a strong desire to heal and protect those less fortunate. I dreamed of joining the Peace Corps. I devoured psychology and philosophy books. The light of Emerson and Thoreau led me through many dark times. In search of the meaning of my life I studied Buddhism, Jung and other religions and philosophies. In college I majored in psychology and I worked in a psychiatric hospital, where I learned their definition of "rehabilitation" was to inject patients with Thorazine and push them through a turnstyle system. My professional purpose wasn't crystallized until I attended The Art Students League in New York City. There I found the camaraderie of artists and my career destiny.

Know thyself.
Socrates

As a young art student, I was challenged by the lack of sufficient opportunities for emerging artists. With a desire to exhibit and show the work of fellow artists I placed a classified ad in the *Village Voice* with a "call to artists." In a few short weeks I had responses from one hundred artists. Inspired by Thomas More's *Utopia* I formed *Artopia*, a multi-media arts organization. In that capacity, I organized exhibitions in a wide variety of alternative spaces and galleries – from Wall Street to Lincoln Center. A singles' club offered me their enormous loft to arrange events that became a popular attraction every weekend. At that time I also joined New York Artists Equity, a vital artists' advocacy organization and served on its Board of Directors to help further artists' rights. Shortly thereafter, a large distribution community newspaper offered me an arts column. I wrote art reviews, without pay, to give emerging artists recognition and establish my position in the New York art world. I quickly learned that being a member of the press is a powerful role, because, everyone wants free publicity.

Dissatisfied that the publications weren't giving me enough of an opportunity to write about emerging artists, in 1983 with the help of my friend and mentor of Harry J. Stathos, a former U.P.I. foreign correspondent I started *Fusion-Arts Review* (which we quickly renamed *Manhattan Arts International*). The cover of the first issue featured the Statue of Liberty as a symbol of freedom. It contained my interview with Jay Leno at the comedy club Caroline's and featured the artwork of many under-recognized artists. Our greatest satisfaction was we helped launch the careers of aspiring visual and performing artists through the publication and the multi-media events we presented in private clubs and cultural centers throughout New York City. *Manhattan Arts International* began as an eight-page newspaper and grew to a four-color magazine with national distribution on newsstands and in galleries and world-wide subscribers.

One of the proudest moments as an artist's advocate was when I organized the Manhattan Arts Debate in 1985 – the only political arts debate in the history of New York City. This event invited the collective art community to raise its voice and ask politicians vital questions through a panel of leaders in the arts. It attracted over 700 guests and received television, radio and print coverage. WQXR, *The New York Times* radio station, broad-casted the event. I realized that as a single individual with a cause I could coordinate something that would motivate others to make a positive difference.

In the late eighties, realizing there was a need for artists to obtain career guidance, I began a career consultation practice and lectured on the business of art in galleries and educational insti-tutions. In 1995 I wrote the first edition of *The Complete Guide to New York Art Galleries*, which further advanced my speaking tours and two other books, including this one.

All of those events led me to exactly where I am, and where I am supposed to be *Now!* Every day I dream, discover, share, create, guide, learn, teach, write, advise and motivate. Every project I pursue is in response to following my music and filling the needs of creative individuals. I am richly rewarded with personal growth. The individuals I serve from around the world are members of my extended family – and my own kind of Peace Corps.

I am blessed with a career that supports me, and yet I never "work." I am privileged to have developed a life of freedom and self-sufficiency in a world where many creative, intelligent individuals are putting their dreams on hold. The concept of waiting until "someday" to begin living a rewarding life, to leave their day job and pursue a career in the arts, is unacceptable. Bob Dylan said: "A man is a success if he gets up in the morning and goes to bed at night and in between does what he wants to do."

I hope you will let me know how this book has helped you find self-sufficiency and joy. I especially look forward to hearing about your success stories.

The most glorious moments in your life
are not the so-called days of success,
but rather those days when
out of dejection and despair
you feel rise in you a challenge to life,
and the promise of future accomplishments.
Gustave Flaubert

CHAPTER 1

IT BEGINS WITH YOU:
THE ARTIST

*If art is to nourish the roots of our culture,
society must set the artist free
to follow his vision wherever it takes him…
We must never forget that art is not a form
of propaganda; it is a form of truth.*
John F. Kennedy

The contemporary art world is a complex and fascinating web of art and commerce. It depends upon a diverse number of individuals, each one contributing in some way by playing a crucial role, none more noticeably important than the other – except for the artist.

The artist's influence on economics – principally the world of real estate – is staggering. Groups of determined artists have been responsible for transforming bleak districts into desirable, posh enclaves, such as SoHo, Tribeca and Chelsea, in New York City, as well as Provincetown, the Hamptons and London's Chelsea, to name a few. However, rather than being supported and revered for their efforts toward renovating, beautifying and financially enriching their environment, their rewards are unjust rent hikes and eventual eviction.

The artist's impact on the economy is immeasurable. The professionals that dependent upon them include art dealers, framers, supply manufacturers, photographers, critics, auctioneers, museum curators and publishers. The artist's impact on civilization is major. If it were not for the artist we would suffer from stagnation, despair and chaos. Without art we would become dehumanized.

Generally speaking,
color directly influences the soul.
Color is the keyboard, the eyes are the hammers,
the soul is the piano with many strings.
The artist is the hand that plays,
touching one key or another purposively,
to cause vibrations in the soul.
Vasily Kandinsky

It begins with you. As an artist you are especially endowed with success. Each day is an opportunity to celebrate the gifts that have been bestowed upon you. You have an acute sensitivity to a myriad of stimuli. You have the power to create something that, before you imagined it, did not exist. With a blank canvas or sheet of paper, a slab of clay, hunk of stone, camera lens, found objects or computer technology, you are capable of bringing inner visions to outer forms. You possess a unique power to elicit a response, alter a person's consciousness and have a major impact on those who see your work and change the course of art history!

That is cause for celebration! You owe it to yourself and to others with every breath you take to use your innate talent to their greatest potential, to claim your voice and to tell your story, to share your gifts and to enrich and deepen our understanding of the human condition.

I paint my own reality. I paint because I need to,
and I paint always whatever passes through my head,
without any other consideration.
Frida Kahlo

MAKE YOUR MARK

Artists are born with a compelling need to probe the depths of self-expression and proclaim self-liberation. The challenge that lies before them is no small task – to explore their innate creativity, fight the demons, ignore the critical voices, discover their strengths, push them to the max, and firmly place their inimitable handprint on the Earth with absolute conviction and no regrets!

When I am asked to examine an artist's work, I look for that handprint – the signs that reveal how the artist has found his or her own voice and has shaped feelings and ideas into unique forms. I always hope to find that *extraordinary* spark of innovation that always makes my heart beat faster.

Art that is noticeably "derivative" of another artist's style and reflects very little of the artist's personal view of the world is a sign that the artist has yet to discover his or her own voice or is afraid to express it. Chuck Close, a major artist of this century, expressed it well when he said that he felt "trapped" in other artists' painting styles, as an abstract expressionist, until he formulated "new ways to make marks that make art."

As an artist you must master your craft and then transcend it: Stop thinking about what others have taught you. Let go of your crutches and fly solo. When you let your unique voice soar you lift the world with you.

I decided I was a very stupid fool
not to at least paint as I wanted to
and say what I wanted to when I painted,
as that seemed to be the only thing I could do
that didn't concern anybody but myself.
Georgia O'Keefe

FOLLOW YOUR PASSION, NOT THE MARKET

Many artists ask me: Which style should I pursue? Where is the market going? They may jump anxiously from one direction to another as if they were chasing the elusive rainbow. I ask them, "What are you most passionate about?" "What do you want to express?" I encourage them to focus on creating their best work first, then their individual market. If they try to guess the market and chase after it by the time they catch it they will be behind it.

If you want to satisfy yourself and build a following I urge you to develop your own signature style. Embrace the subjects, colors, textures, ideas, experiences, shapes and events that resonate most strongly to you. Follow your muse, bring your inspiration to fruition and take that to the bank with pride!

Wolf Kahn, a highly esteemed artist, teacher and writer on art, who has exhibited at the Whitney Museum of American Art, says in the book *Wolf Kahn's America,* "I run the risk of being considered a barn painter. I do like painting barns, all the while worrying that I paint them because it is expected of me. I have had art dealers come into my studio, asking first thing, 'Got any barns?' My innate perversity saves me. That, and the knowledge that, to be an artist, one shouldn't merely fulfill expectations."

Fulfilling expectations can be a problem when it threatens creative freedom. For several years Bob's gallery was generating steady sales of his abstract paintings. He wanted to change artistic directions but feared he would lose income and status if he did. His new passion was a series of animal paintings inspired by volunteer work in an animal protection organization. His concern was he would have to choose between creative freedom and financial security.

During the consultation I reassured Bob he didn't have to make a choice. With some well-developed strategies he began to feel assured that he could achieve both within a comfortable period of time. Armed with a plan Bob's worries dissipated and he experienced a burst of creative energy. He completed several paintings ahead of our schedule and forged ahead with our marketing campaign that led to several commissions and national press. An introduction to a product licensor expanded sales into the giftware industry. He gained two new galleries and the gallery that sold his abstract paintings accepted his new work.

When you trust your creative voice the art will speak. During a very painful period in her life – after learning about her husband's infidelity – Beverly was propelled into creating a patchwork quilt. Each patch expressed a different emotion that she experienced during the process of her divorce. It took several months, but with each stitch her rage came pouring out. Her art liberated her from her pain. Afterward, selling the quilt finalized the process of letting go. More empowered than ever before, she moved on with her life. She had turned pain into power, passion and profit.

To become truly immortal a work of art
must escape all human limits:
logic and common sense will only interfere.
Once these barriers are broken it will enter the regions
of childhood vision and dream.
Giorgio de Chirico

Dare To Dream

As creative individuals we know that we live in two worlds – the waking world that abides by logic and science and the mysterious world of dreaming. In the dream world we may experience surrealistic events, view fantastic images and undergo profound transformations. It is known that probably everyone dreams, although many of us forget most or all of them. There seem to be more questions than answers on this subject of which much has been studied and written. Scientists know that normally we dream for about one fifth of the time that we are asleep. Just imagine – there is an abundance of inspirational symbols, messages and references waiting to be revealed to us as we lay our heads on our pillows.

We know that many artists have received their creative ideas from their dreams. Great painters such as the Italian Surrealist Giorgio de Chirico and the Belgium Surrealist Paul Delvaux were known to capture the dream phases of their lives and combined familiar images in bizarre contexts. The noted Spanish Surrealist Salvador Dali not only aspired to remember the exact details of his dream landscapes but he actually strove to induce them. As exciting as it may seem many individuals feel uncomfortable about delving into this mysterious world and self-conscious about revealing their subconscious.

Barbara's portfolio contained fifty paintings. The most provocative among them was a painting that contained an extraordinary creature that nearly leapt from the canvas. I asked her what inspired this engaging, surreal life form. At first she was reluctant to open up, but later with some embarrassment she told me her it originated from her dreams. She created many paintings of it, but was afraid to show them and removed them from her portfolio. She said, "These paintings are strange. People will think I'm crazy. No one will want to buy them."

We continued to discuss her imaginary creature and I recommended some books on the power of dreams on art and dream interpretation. She agreed to let this creature evolve and in time she translated more of her dream images into a magnificent and prolific body of work. The positive responses she started to receive, including sales and awards, erased her embarrassment. She discovered the tremendous power of dreams, the joyful process of creative freedom, and she came to trust her unique vision. By exploring the unknown and having the courage to risk derision, Barbara also developed more confidence in her personal life. She accepted and honored the creative child within her that had been thwarted by judgment and ridicule.

Are dreams a revelation from some profound creative source within ourselves? Through the ages the meaning of dreams and their significance have intrigued humankind. The most ancient civilizations believed that dreams carried messages from the gods. Although scientists tend to agree that there must be a purpose to dreaming, they disagree over what this purpose might be. Dream research is one of the areas where the layperson is as competent as the professional. It requires no special equipment beyond a notebook and pencil to begin the exploration and discovery. There are many books on the subject that are written to help us understand and interpret our dreams as well as understand more about ourselves. Dreams can provide powerful tools.

The great Indian mystic and physician Patanjali, who lived somewhere between 200 B.C. and 200 A.D., and who first recognized the power in the practice of meditation, said, "When you are inspired by some great purpose, some extraordinary project, all your thoughts break their bonds; your mind transcends limitations, your consciousness expands in every direction, and you find yourself in a new, great and wonderful world. Dormant forces, faculties and talents become alive, and you discover yourself to be a greater person by far than you ever dreamed yourself to be."

Trust the power of your passion and subconscious. As you venture deeply into the world of introspection there are many discoveries about yourself waiting to be revealed. Your art is a reflection of how you respond to life – your emotions, your experiences, your values, beliefs and choices – the sum of what makes you unique. Let it shine. Let it rejoice. Let it reverberate throughout the world. Let it shock. Let it rock. Let it console. Let it cajole. Let it break all the rules. Let it claim new frontiers. Let it flood the universe. Let it make a ruckus. Let it fill the air with song. Let it be.

The minute I sat in front of a canvas, I was happy.
Because it was a world, and I could do as I like in it.
Alice Neel

CHAPTER 2

FIVE KEYS TO SUCCESS

If you develop the habits of success,
you will make success a habit.
Michael E. Angier

Over the years, I've studied the behavior of many artists and I've observed certain traits are consistent with those who attain their goals with fewer difficulties. The traits I find to be most valuable are not talent, education or wealth – they are confidence, commitment, persistence and the ability to develop and manage change.

CONFIDENCE

One of the reasons why many artists reserve a private consultation with me is to be reassured that they have talent. They want to know whether they are wasting their time on a dream that may never come to fruition – of being a successful artist. Someone like me who can offer objective, professional feedback and can point out an artist's strengths and offer encouragement is helpful. But, unless the artist is deeply convinced of his or her own abilities, the temporary boost of confidence will fade at the first sign of rejection. I am often asked: "Do you ever tell an artist to give up their art?" My answer is "never!" I take pleasure in encouraging individuals to find their passion, increase their confidence and apply commitment. Many determined artists who others may judge as being untalented deserve to attain personal satisfaction and commercial success. I admire anyone who has talent but I also respect the person who has a burning desire to achieve.

If you think you can, you can.
And, if you think you can't, you're right.
Mary Kay Ash

When you watch an Olympic champion, you can see their intense concentration and belief in their ability to excel, and how it propels them forward. The best competitor knows that the smallest doubt will encumber his or her performance.

Beth is a very talented artist with a magnetic personality. She has spurts of confidence and energy followed by bouts of inertia and depression. She chooses men who squash her self-confidence. She doesn't exhibit her work because she feels it isn't good enough. When she has a professional interview she suffers from loss of sleep and anxiety, which lead to poor creativity. Beth has a tremendous potential to excel, however, until she builds self-esteem she will continue to underachieve.

Developing confidence is like building muscles. You may not always *feel* confident, but if you learn how to *act* confident when you need to, your behavior will affect your attitude. You know the expression, "fake it 'till you make it." When you feel shaky stand erect and speak with conviction. Visualize a time when you felt self-assured and recreate that feeling.

Every achievement is tangible proof that you are capable of attaining any goal you desire. When you accomplish a measure of success, give yourself the proverbial pat on the back. Frame your awards, letters of acceptances and positive reviews and display them within your view.

You gain strength, courage and confidence by every experience
in which you really stop to look fear in the face.
You are able to say to yourself, "I lived through this horror.
I can take the next thing that comes along."
You must do the thing you think you cannot do.
Eleanor Roosevelt

COMMITMENT

When your career is going smoothly, it is easy to stay committed to your goals. When sales are steady, you seem to attract more buyers. When your work receives rave reviews, you are inspired to produce. Then – wham! Without warning, your art gets damaged in a flood, your gallery goes bankrupt, you fall and break your wrist or the promised fellowship or grant falls through. You may be tempted to give up – but don't! Success is not measured in terms of a single event but our endurance to prevail. We triumph when we face the tragic events in our lives.

Physical prowess, financial wealth or intelligence will not help you as much as commitment. Chuck Close, one of the world's most respected artists, knew he wanted to be an artist from the age of four. He learned about commitment when, despite learning disabilities he persevered and went on to college. Later as an established artist he was struck with a sudden near-fatal illness. He is now quadriplegic and sits in a wheel chair with a brush strapped to his wrist to paint his inimitable magnificent, large paintings. In the book *Chronicles of Courage* by Jean Kennedy Smith and George Plimpton, he states: "One thing that was clear to me early on was how important it was to have something to do – something that you're anxious to get back to. I wanted to get back to work because I enjoy what I do. I love making art... It's largely how I see myself. I'm an artist, therefore I have to make art."

Until one is committed, there is hesitancy,
the chance to draw back, always ineffectiveness.
Concerning all acts of initiative, there is one elementary truth, the
ignorance of which kills countless ideas and splendid plans:
That the moment one definitely commits oneself,
then providence moves too... Whatever you can do, or dream you
can, begin it. Boldness has genius, power, and magic in it.
Goethe

Having a steadfast commitment to a dream means following through with hourly, daily, weekly and monthly goals. It means making sacrifices, setting priorities, taking risks and investing substantial amounts of time and effort.

Mark di Suvero is one of the best-known sculptors in the world. Early in his career he was crushed in an elevator under a one-ton weight. He has found a way to crawl inside a crane in order to lift several tons of weight to make his fifty-foot sculptures. Since his accident his pieces have constantly grown in scale. In the book *Chronicles of Courage* di Suvero is quoted as saying: "The more of yourself you put into it, the more you get out... Anyone who creates art for any length of time ends up with this wish to bring more to the world!"

As you know for an artist art is oxygen for the soul. If you are dedicated to being a professional artist, no matter how busy you are, never put your art on the back burner. Make time for creating your art. Commitment will help you develop a strong, cohesive body of work – an important feature when you bring your art to the public. Dealers look for art that has an aesthetic similitude – a solid, mature artistic vision. In an essay in *The New Criterion*, renowned artist Alex Katz wrote: "It takes most painters at least eight or ten years to master the craft and become proficient, and perhaps another eight or ten years to become a master."

Persistence

Any artist who finally achieves a major breakthrough in their career will tell you they worked very hard and devotedly for many years. They didn't give up after the first phone call wasn't returned or when several galleries rejected their work.

Native New York painter E. Jay Weiss is an artist-in residence of the beautifully renovated Cabrini Hospice Inpatient Unit in Manhattan, where patients dealing with end of life issues are surrounded by a world-class art installation which E. Jay designed and curated. For nearly four decades he has persisted in making a living from his work despite a rejection file that, he says, "...reads like a *Who's Who* of art dealers and galleries." In 1993, he suffered a crippling injury while working and subsequently gave up more than one home and studio. Having to put his possessions and his life's work in storage for years at a time (at one point he recalls having to move eighteen times in as many months), he carried his materials with him and produced work that led him beyond those limitations. His paintings often reveal enclosed limitlessness; the artist weaves layers of liquid paint that resonate a structured infinitude of light and depth.

After September 11, 2001 E. Jay dedicated a year painting a thirty-five foot; nine panel elegy. In 2002, an accident on his way to "Ground Zero" aggravated his previous injury and he had to finish the series of paintings on crutches. In that emergency, after thirty-two years of applying for artist grants, he was assisted by grants from both the New York Foundation for the Arts and the Gottlieb Foundation. The nine-panel "9-11 ELEGY: GHOST CITY" paintings began a tour of exhibitions in the New York City area and led to the artist being awarded a Pollock-Krasner Foundation Grant for painting in 2003. E. Jay Weiss currently lives and works and thrives in his studio in Chelsea.

As a career consultant I am often asked to help artists promote their exhibitions. It was around September 20, shortly after the World Trade Center tragedy, when Ronaldo hired us to promote his major one-person exhibition. We culled a large database, developed presentation materials, called the people in our database, left many messages, mailed materials, and followed up with more calls. At a time when many business people were in a state of inertia many of our calls went unanswered, but we persisted. One call to a publicist revealed a need for a sculpture for a campaign. The timing was perfect and the project generated a windfall of income and publicity for Ronaldo.

Persistence is required to bring your art to the public, through exhibitions and media exposure. It is important to stay focused and visible so that a large population of people will become accustomed to you and your style. Tenacity will build your résumé and a strong résumé is perceived as being professional, dependable and marketable. On the contrary, a résumé with several interruptions raises questions and doubts about whether you are a serious artist.

The next time you feel like giving up remember these examples of persistence: The Coca-Cola company sold only four hundred Cokes in its first year of business and Dr. Seuss's first book was rejected by twenty-three publishers.

> *Courage is doing what you're afraid to do.*
> *There can be no courage unless you're scared.*
> Eddie Rickenbacker

COURAGE

Fear often discourages us from stretching and testing new grounds and reaching our potential. When we are afraid to fail we may set only a few minor goals or none at all. William Shakespeare said, "Our doubts are traitors, and make us lose the good we oft might win, by fearing to attempt."

Michael is a talented artist from California who has tremendous courage. He integrates painting, sculpture and digital art. He has vision impairment from CMV Retinitis and AIDS, yet he has overcome many obstacles by having a positive attitude and tremendous motivation. Between eye surgeries when his vision fails him he creates sculpture. When his funding runs low he applies for more grants. He continuously searches for help. He is determined to prevent any ailment threaten his need to express himself and share his art with the world. Michael is an inspiration for us to have the courage to set very high goals.

Develop a thirst for getting out of your comfort zone. Take risks, especially in the face of defeat. Begin by taking one chance each day. Make the phone call, arrange the appointment, throw the paint onto the canvas, break the mold. Living as an artist is living in the excitement of not knowing what idea or venture will come to you next, or how. The moment you know how, you begin to lose creative spontaneity. Take chances and leaps of faith in the shrouds of mystery.

The real voyage of discovery consists not in seeking new landscapes, but in having new eyes.
Marcel Proust

CHANGE

Charles Darwin said: "It is not the strongest of the species that survive, nor the most intelligent, but the one most responsive to change." The Irish playwright George Bernard Shaw reminded us, "Progress is impossible without change, and those who cannot change their minds cannot change anything."

When you hear the popping of champagne corks with the dawn of a new year, do you feel the excitement of entering an exciting, new realm of unlimited possibilities or does the fear of the unknown paralyze you?

When you begin a clean slate, take a good long look at the past year. What did you learn from your experiences? What changes could you make to correct your mistakes?

Expect relapse. Psychology experts consider relapse part of the process of change. Reports have said most people who succeeded in keeping their New Year's resolutions slip at least a dozen times. Focus on one change at a time and don't expect immediate results. It takes at least one month to make a new habit automatic.

Don't dwell on your mistakes. Focus on your accomplishments, applaud yourself for making all of the wise decisions you made, and continue to take the same positive action that brought you success. Which tactics did you apply that were most effective? What must you continue to do in order to increase your achievements?

The human tendency prefers familiar horrors to unknown delights.
Fred Woodworth

Change has a considerable psychological impact on the human mind. To the fearful it is threatening because it suggests things might get worse. A person's character and frame of mind determines how receptive he or she is to making changes and how he or she reacts when change is imposed.

To be successful in our very fast-paced, volatile environment we need to be aware of the changes occurring every day in the worlds of economy, business, politics, communication, technology and education – all of which impact the artist.

If you want eternal youth and vitality, embrace change with a positive attitude. Stay abreast of emerging trends, new art forms, techniques, new ways of exhibiting and marketing your art and new "artspeak." Read leading-edge art magazines from around the globe. Avoid the temptation to immediately dismiss anything new and different. Look for new ways to bring your art to new audiences. Surround yourself with youthful, innovative and exuberant people who welcome change.

Heraculitus said: "Nothing endures but change." As your life changes, so will your goals and priorities. A periodic checkup will help you to see if your life's purpose and current situation are complementary. It is important to ask yourself periodically: "Am I pursuing my goals *Now*? Do I feel passionate about the kind of art I am producing *Now*? These questions will either comfort you or provoke you to make profound changes.

Things do not change; we change.

Henry David Thoreau

21 POWERFUL QUESTIONS THAT INSPIRE CHANGE

1. What does "success" mean to me?
2. What are my priorities today? This year? This lifetime?
3. What positive step can I take *Now!* to achieve success?
4. How am I procrastinating and why?
5. Am I currently creating what my heart tells me to?
6. What toxic relationship or materials should I avoid?
7. How am I sabotaging my career?
8. How much money do I want to earn this year from my art?
9. How can I channel my talent to serve humanity?
10. Who deserves an apology from me? Gratitude? Forgiveness?
11. How do I want to be remembered?
12. Which new medium should I explore or invent?
13. How can I push my art to a higher level?
14. What should I be teaching others about art and artists?
15. Am I in a state of inertia and need help?
16. What are my strengths?
17. How well do I manage difficulties and challenges?
18. What would happen if I changed my career path?
19. How is my state of mind impacting my career development?
20. Am I taking responsibility for my shortcomings?
21. What new skills and information do I need and where can I acquire them?

CHAPTER 3

CREATE YOUR MASTER PLAN & PLAN YOUR DESTINY

He who controls others may be powerful,
but he who has mastered himself is mightier still.
Lao Tsu

It is easy to become distracted by the daily routine of life that we lose sight of our dreams. Misplaced priorities, lack of will or the fear of failure takes us on a path that is far away from where we planned to be. An article in *The New York Times* reported a survey conducted by umbershoot.net, a web site for discussing ideas. It revealed: "Many of the people who seem to have it 'all' harbor dreams about the road not taken." Among chief executives, 47% said their life-long dream was to be a sculptor. Imagine that!

We all have a mission in life – one that gives our life meaning and purpose. It is a total manifestation of our unique capabilities and heartfelt desires. Our mission is profoundly more than our role as artist, parent, spouse, teacher or writer. We often make the mistake of defining ourselves by our role, which limits our potential. We often fail to see the larger picture.

Your choice to be an artist is part of your mission, but what *kind* of artist do you want to be? What do you want to *do* with your art? What kind of *impact* do you want your art to make? If you were to write your eulogy, what would it say? How are you going to be remembered? What values did you express? How did you change the lives of others? How were you unique?

Mandela's mission was to end apartheid; Mother Teresa's mission was to offer solace to the sick and end human suffering. Few of us will ever accomplish what they did but you can still achieve remarkable things. Your art can serve as a catalyst if your mission is to participate in social change. It can provide solace for broken hearts if your mission is to heal. It can be the stimulus for tolerance among different cultures if your mission is to unite. Embrace those big dreams that seem elusive and integrate them into your daily habits to make them tangible. What action could you take right *Now!* that would set your dream in motion? Create your master plan and plan your destiny.

We act as though comfort and luxury
were the chief requirements of life,
when all that we need to
make us happy is something to be enthusiastic about.
Charles Kingsley

All great journeys begin with a desired destination. As a career consultant I have learned that at the root of many career problems lies uncertainty, a feeling of powerlessness and a lack of direction. When a client comes to me for guidance my desire is to help them attain focus, self-sufficiency and empowerment. Before the consultation begins, I ask them to provide, along with their presentation materials, a list of their objectives. I usually ask, "Where do you want to be one or two years from now?"

This helps them to define their goals, establish their priorities, identify their strengths and take charge of their careers. The process helps them tune into their values, their view of themselves, their expectations and so much more. From that vantage point we can pursue a tremendous range of possibilities, opportunities, plans and strategies.

Shoot for the moon.
Even if you miss it you will land among the stars.
Les Brown

As soon as you establish what you truly desire, you can prepare your goals, strategies and activities. If you reverse the order, you may find yourself very preoccupied with "To Do" lists without deriving satisfaction from your busy activities. Personal harmony is more important than achieving status or prosperity.

Strive to attain balance between your creative, career and financial goals. Examine your personal values and preferences and determine if they are compatible with your goals. Are you happier with the randomness of change or the security of a routine? Do you prefer to work with a team of creative individuals or are you happiest when working alone? Do you enjoy the rush of frequent deadlines or do you feel more comfortable when working at a slower pace? How much creative freedom are you willing to sacrifice in order to gain financial success? Do you have what is required to be a full-time Artrepreneur? Be sure your goals are truly what you want and not what somebody else thinks you should attain. Avoid confusing the values and goals of those in your sphere of influence with your own.

Success *Now!* means that you hold the key to your own success, the moment you decide to believe in your ability to create your destiny. Success comes as you begin moving toward a worthwhile goal. I recommend spending at least 30 minutes alone in the beginning of each day quietly focusing on your goals. You may want to record them in your own voice.

Picture yourself vividly as winning
and that alone will contribute immeasurably to success.
Great living starts with a picture,
held in your imagination, of what you would like to be.
Dr. Harry Emerson Fosdick

VISUALIZE YOUR GOALS

As a creative individual, you have powerful perceptions. Use your gift of imagination to activate a four dimensional picture of your desired goals. Surround yourself with positive affirmations, talented people, great books, music, posters and collages describing your goals in rich, vivid pictures, words and sounds.

Create a Dream Book, and fill it with pictures of your ideal home, spacious studio, dream exhibition or performance space, adventurous foreign lands, heavenly artists' retreats and other delights that you want to attract into your life. Post your favorite pictures, positive images and inspiring quotes on your studio wall, bathroom mirror, above your desk, in your wallet – places where you will see them everyday. Frame and hang your certificates of awards and letters of acceptances as a reminder of how it feels to be a winner.

If your goal is to use your art to heal children inflicted with major illnesses visualize every detail of the project, the people who will be participating and the places you will be bringing your work. If your goal is to build your own studio near a body of water start make sketches of it and collect pictures and articles from the real estate sections of newspapers and magazines.

Great minds have purposes; others simply have wishes.
Washington Irving

YOUR CAREER GOALS

Ponder the words of Dr. Robert Schuller: "What would you attempt to do if you knew you could not fail?" Would you quit your job and become a full-time artist? Would you move to Europe and sculpt huge pieces in marble? Would you open a gallery with fellow artists? Would you start an art program, foundation, art school or art organization?

Carl Sandburg said, "Nothing happens unless first a dream." Once you have envisioned your dream as your goal, foresee any barriers and obstacles that may appear and develop alternative plans and solutions. Determine where the hurdles are by asking: What is stopping me from having my goals met? How will achieving my goal affect other areas in my life? What are the positive and negative consequences of reaching my aspirations? What resources do I already have, and what additional resources do I need in order to accomplish my goals?

Give your dream wings. Be your best agent. Spread the word. Give your goals a voice. Tell your friends, relatives and other artists about your desires and talents and business ventures and ask them to share the news with others. Joseph Campbell said, "If you are on the right path you will find that invisible hands are helping." Knowing that family, friends, business partners or the entire world is cheering for us, counting on us and supporting us is critically important. Befriend an artist or a group of artists with the goal of encouraging each other to stay on track, especially during difficult setbacks. Do you know anyone who does *not* want you to succeed? If so, sever the connection or at least keep them at a distance.

> *To know oneself, one should assert oneself.*
> Albert Camus

Take one step forward each day. Make the phone call, write the letter or attend the event. Ask some questions to get started. What do I want to achieve today? What specific task needs to get done today? Be willing to change self-sabotaging habits that lead you off your course. Create new goal plans periodically, and set higher ones with each triumph. Be flexible. When one plan doesn't work, try another! Don't try to be "Superperson." Examine your energy levels over a period of a few weeks. Set realistic and reasonable time frames in accordance to those levels.

Once you know what you need to accomplish proceed with relentless determination. When Susan made the commitment to finish several new paintings for her one-person exhibition, I advised her to clear her schedule of everything non-essential for two weeks. She told her friends she wouldn't be available for telephone chats during the day and prepared a few meals ahead for her family and put them in the freezer. She spent eight hours a day in her studio and refused to allow any distractions interrupt her. At the end of two weeks she felt victorious and was prepared for a successful show!

The word affluence means "to flow in abundance."
So, let prosperity flow to you.

YOUR FINANCIAL GOALS

Professional power increases with financial security. The first step to obtaining prosperity is determining the amount of money you need to live the kind of lifestyle you desire.

Be specific. It is not sufficient to say: "I want fame and fortune." What is your definition of fame and fortune? What amount of money and kind of lifestyle would make you happy? How would you spend, share and invest your money?

Will your earnings come from being a full-time artist or supplemented from another source? Have you determined the actual dollar amount you want to earn in order to establish security as a full-time artist? Did you create your business plan? *(See the chapter on Taking Care of Business.)* Are you satisfied with last year's income? What steps will you take to improve your financial situation next year? What have you learned from the goals you did not reach?

If you want to reach your financial goals the first step is to do some calculations. List your financial goal for the coming year. Decide how many works of art you will need to sell in order to reach that goal. If your annual goal is $50,000 sales of your artwork, and your average selling price is $500, you will need about 100 sales. In order to reach those prospects, you will need to invest time, effort and money, such as in exhibition expenses, direct mail, marketing and promotion.

Creative decisions also have to be made according to your working methods. If you create sculpture or paintings that require extensive work and you can only complete one or two each year, you need a different set of financial goals than a more prolific artist who has a larger inventory to sell.

Painter, it is better to be rich than poor:
so learn how to make gold and precious stones
come out of your brush.
Salvador Dali

MONEY IS GREEN POWER

Finance is often a difficult subject to discuss with an artist. Money is a very sensitive issue and carries a hefty weight of emotional baggage. Take, for example, an artist who is financially dependent upon her or his spouse. Questions about need, self-worth and self-sufficiency can interfere with an artist's career if not addressed properly and if solutions are not found.

Catharine came to me for a consultation at the end of the calendar year. Her financial situation was definitely a priority of concern, as she and her husband had a recent conversation over the fact that she hadn't sold any work in the previous year. He told her he could allocate only $1,500 toward her career in the next year.

We could have spent her consultation time solving Catharine's immediate restriction of working on a $1,500 allowance. Instead, I chose to work on a greater, more meaningful challenge. We discussed her attitude about her career, her relationship with money and the value she placed on her art. She saw herself as being dependent upon her husband and felt guilty about the $1,500 he was giving her. Without making some major changes, she would probably return the following year with the same problem or worse.

First, we took out Catharine's presentation materials and evaluated their strength as her "sales force." We agreed she needed better quality visuals and her résumé needed to be rewritten to emphasize her career achievements.

We examined her use of time. I advised her to withdraw her membership from the small unprofessional art group that was insufficient in helping to advance her career. Instead, I encouraged her to apply for more selective exhibitions juried by museum curators. They would lead to better credentials, higher visibility and more sales.

Experience is not what happens to a (wo)man,
it is what a (wo)man does with what happens...
Aldous Huxley

I encouraged Catharine to take a more assertive approach about her career. She promised to communicate to relatives and associates that her art was available for sale, and ask them for help in spreading the word. She would accept her aunt's offer to host a soirée in her apartment with some of Catharine's paintings. She also applied for some grants. She agreed to practice networking by strengthening the contacts she already had in addition to building relationships with new business prospects such as interior designers and architects in her area. I augmented her prospects with a mailing list of corporate art consultants and curators. We created a small but attractive brochure.

It was time to discuss her prices. She showed me a list of thirty works available for sale. I thought the prices were too high. We agreed to adjust them and consider raising them in six months. It was important to build a loyal customer base and sales history and move the inventory of paintings out of the studio to make room for future works. Instead of going into debt we decided to use some of her work to barter for framing, photography, equipment and printing. The total of the remaining inventory came to $15,000 and I said, "Look at this list as $15,000 waiting to be collected. How long it takes will depend on you."

Catharine was exhilarated to learn that financial independence was in her grasp. She began transforming the view she had of herself, her relationships and her career. Her self-esteem gave her fresh ideas to increase steady income, such as giving art instructions to children each Saturday, which supplemented her monthly income with $800. She found a way to work on small paintings of her own while she taught the children. She also learned how to turn the students' parents into her collectors!

Like Catharine many artists are so intimidated by the idea of managing their money that it paralyzes their creativity. Don't let that happen to you. Get comfortable with money, know how much you have, how to use it and make it grow. Make it your partner. Suze Orman, financial expert and best selling author says, "Money has no power of its own." Catharine learned how to fuel money with "Green Power" and change dependency into self-reliance.

The ideal artist is the superman.
He uses every possible power, spirit, emotion –
conscious or unconscious – to arrive at his ends.
George Bellows

A goal is a dream with deadlines.

YOUR ACTION PLAN: AN EXERCISE

Action plans consist of desires, goals, strategies and activities. An example of a desire might be to acquire a larger, separate studio. The goal might be to earn $50,000 this year from sales of your work. A strategy might be to increase sales through corporate art consultants. Activities might be: purchase a mailing list; make appointments with ten corporate art consultants next month; and design a new brochure by April. Target dates and lists help you stay on course and get the job done on time.

SAMPLE

<u>Desire:</u> To become financially self-sufficient and improve my family's lifestyle.

<u>Goal:</u> Increase art sales from $15,000 to $50,000 during the next two years.

<u>Strategy:</u> Build more sales outlets through interior designers, architects and individuals.

<u>Activities:</u> Prepare a sales brochure.

<u>Target Dates:</u>   June 14: Finish the design
July 1: Send to printer
August 12: Mail brochure

<u>To Do List:</u>
> Review brochure samples from my file.
> Call Jim, graphic designer. Make appointment to discuss brochure design.
> Hire photographer for new works.

YOUR ACTION PLAN FOR
CREATIVE, CAREER & FINANCIAL GOALS

Desire: _____
_____
_____
_____

Creative / Career / Financial Goal: _____
_____
_____
_____

Strategy: _____
_____
_____
_____

Activities: _____
_____
_____
_____

Target Dates: _____
_____
_____
_____

To Do List: _____
_____
_____
_____

What information do you need? Where can you go to get what
you need? Who will be your role models? Do you need a career
coach?

CHAPTER 4

MYTHS, FAIRY TALES & SELF-SABOTAGE

If you could kick the person
responsible for most of your troubles,
you would not be able to sit down for months.
Unknown

When we examine why artists are besieged by frustration, we don't have to look far for causes – the insensitive parents that discourage them from pursuing their dreams, the government's frequent apathy toward the Arts, the traditional educational system that fails to prepare the artist for the realities of the professional art world, and the discrimination against women and other minorities – to name a few.

For centuries artists have had to endure many obstacles, and in recent years since art has become big business, it is often difficult to circumvent them and find the doorways to opportunities. Many artists who are unprepared to function effectively in the business of art become enraged and cynical toward this imperfect, unfair system of competition, demands, controls and power struggles. They resent having to be subservient to the individuals they have to depend on for support. Their defense is either to lash out at the commercial establishment or retreat to an idealized fantasy world where they imagine someone will come to their rescue. If artists don't utilize healthy forms of coping such as becoming art advocates or changing the system from within these harsh realities may disable and stifle their creative, career and financial potential.

> *As long as a man stands in his own way,*
> *everything seems to be in his way.*
> Ralph Waldo Emerson

Many artists waste tremendous energy waging war on too many trivial fronts and pursuing lost causes. Instead of making adversaries it is more important to attract allies. Energy can be wasted on agonizing over what *cannot* be changed in the outside reality. Looking within for direction is more constructive. Sometimes self-sabotage may be the larger obstacle.

Artists sabotage themselves when they behave overly sensitive to criticism, when they refuse to take the responsibility for their careers, and when they cling to bitterness. They sabotage their careers when they use inferior materials to create their work, submit poor quality slides to a jury or mail their show invitations too late. They are their own worst enemies when they show blatant disrespect toward another professional or enter a relationship with an abusive dealer.

In spite of the challenges many artists have learned to thrive in the business of being an artist. They adopt a realistic and positive outlook. They accept responsibility for their own successes and failures, and they empower themselves with education, camaraderie and business skills.

The path to success begins by rejecting the myths that have poisoned artists for centuries perpetuating the notion that artists are subservient to dealers, collectors and critics. Many artists have been harmed because they have accepted such myths and stereotypes as, "I'm An Artist, Not A Business Person", "The Poor Starving Artist", and "Someday My Prince(ss) Will Come."

Every human being on this earth
is born with a tragedy, and it isn't original sin.
He's born with the tragedy that he has to grow up.
A lot of people don't have the courage to do it.
Helen Hayes

"I'M AN ARTIST, NOT A BUSINESSPERSON"

"I can't handle the business tasks!" many artists will exclaim, as if it were a dreadful disease that will contaminate their artistic abilities. The very thoughts of drafting a business plan, creating presentation materials or contacting galleries make their creative juices freeze.

The fact that most artists today are unprepared for the professional art world is not entirely their fault. For centuries, they have been told that they lack business sophistication. It is only recently that art business courses have been offered to artists to assist them, although these limited courses are not required. Unfortunately, artists graduate with a misguided fantasy that someone else will be responsible for preparing written documents, dealing with the press, insuring, marketing and selling their art, along with contacting galleries, museums and art consultants, and fulfilling the other obligations to further their careers. When they learn the truth it shocks them and, without survival skills, their hopes dissolve very quickly. They believe the only avenue open to them is to wait on tables, teach art or work in the commercial art field – without ever escaping.

It is important to avoid thinking in terms of situations being either black or white. Taking care of business does not mean you have to sacrifice creativity and being an artist does not disable you from comprehending business principles. In fact, the best entrepreneurs – in any field – are those individuals who strive for balance and exercise a creative approach to solving problems. Creative people are naturally strong in areas that are important for business success, such as developing concepts, using flexibility, learning new skills and having the ability to handle many tasks at one time.

It takes time and patience to develop new skills. You may have to take baby steps at first but when you master them and reap the benefits you will want to take on greater challenges.

One can never consent to creep
when one feels an impulse to soar.
Helen Keller

Early in my artistic career, I was naïve, impatient and idealistic. With the help of an unpleasant experience in a summer job I gained some maturity and an improved sense of reality. I took a part-time job for an established fashion designer in The Hamptons whose clients were celebrities and socialites. She laid bolts of silks and cottons on a table, and my task was to paint my own color designs on them with acrylic paint.

My work area was a hot, tiny, crowded room in the back of this posh boutique but it was easy for me to escape into the joyful process of creativity. As I painted I imagined how the wearable art would adorn the people who wore them. As time passed I became very skillful and fast. One day, I painted an entire wedding party ensemble – from hats to shoes!

After my work was completed, the designer signed her name to the apparel. I overheard the clients in the front of the store praising her. Sure, my ego was sorely bruised, and I was tempted many times to quit the job, but I had a good reason to stay. The compensation I received for one day's work paid the entire month's rent on my own studio where I had the freedom to create paintings and sign my name. I recognized that the short-term sacrifice helped me reach my long-term goal.

Very few people know how to work.
Inspiration, everybody has inspiration, that's just hot air.
Beatrice Wood

I decided to become a student of business and learn from the designer. In this boutique I took my first steps to self-sufficiency. I learned about the importance of using money as a tool. I learned if I wanted to avoid being subservient to others I would have to gain business skills, promote myself and earn a reputation of my own. The next summer, in addition to selling my paintings on canvas, I had my own hand painted line of apparel known as "Renée's Originals" which sold in several boutiques on Long Island.

You will encounter many people along the way who will teach you in surprising ways. Select mentors and role models whom you want to emulate. Learn about the business of art by reading the biographies of successful artists and the many informative art and business books available today. Take courses and attend lectures that offer practical solutions to your specific career challenges.

Everything you need you already have.
You are complete right now, you are a whole,
total person, not an apprentice person
on the way to someplace else.
Your completeness must be understood by you
and experienced in your thoughts
as your own personal reality.
Wayne W. Dyer

"THE POOR, STARVING ARTIST"

It is time to bury this myth! For decades, it has served to create an aura of romance and mystique, which helps to market books and art by artists who have more value to art sellers through their posthumous reputations. The negative stereotype of the pathetic, neurotic artist living in an unkempt garret, eating sardines and stale bread, and drinking cheap wine, victimizes all living artists. It robs them of their power to prosper with dignity. Rather than hearing about Vincent van Gogh's malaise or about how many artists have died from AIDS and drug abuse, I prefer to discuss success stories about artists who have shattered this myth and forged a path to prosperity and independence. Bravo to those who have replaced "The Poor, Starving Artist" with "The Self-Empowered Artist."

There are times when you may think that you must be crazy to have chosen this profession. Members of your family may proclaim that you are naïve and immature, and ask you, "When will you give up your obsession and pursue a *real* career?" Edouard Manet probably heard such ridicule when he was destined for law but chose to study painting despite parental opposition. Ironically, there are many attorneys, accountants and engineers who are on the unemployment line, but I've never heard anyone refer to them as "The Poor, Starving Attorney." Hopefully, you have learned to ignore such questions and find the courage to be a non-conformist. Follow your creative path with confidence and determination, and avoid the trap of self-destruction and shame.

There is only one success –
to be able to spend your life in your own way.
Christopher Morley

The term, "The Poor, Starving Artist," is in truth an oxymoron because the artist is richly rewarded and fulfilled from creating something that originates from his or her inner spirit. Today, many individuals who once thought material wealth was the path to nirvana are experiencing depression and anxiety, starving for identity and job satisfaction. Striving for money, fame, popularity and position without a spiritual foundation has led to an epidemic of soul hunger that the plethora of self-help books are trying to fill.

It is unfortunate that many artists fall prey to the self-fulfilling prophesy of the being "The Poor, Starving Artist." They may identify with this image to avoid taking responsibility and behaving maturely. If they see themselves as helpless victims they will never know the rich rewards of self-empowerment.

The consuming desire of most human beings
is deliberately to plant their whole life
in the hands of some other person.
I would describe this method of searching
for happiness as immature.
Development of character consists solely
in moving toward self-sufficiency.
Quentin Crisp

"SOMEDAY MY PRINCE(SS) WILL COME"

Wouldn't it be nice to hear the proverbial tap on your studio door from the magnanimous patron or benevolent art dealer, who has come to take care of you with large sales, important collectors, rave reviews and one-person shows? And, all you had to do in return was spend your time creating art?

That's the dream of many artists I've met. The illusion of Sleeping Beauty is much more appealing than the reality of being an artist, but it is pragmatism that builds personal power. You know the lyrics: "Fairy tales can come true, they can happen to you..." But let me add: "...if you're willing to commit your self to hard work." Artists are "discovered" after many years of acquiring artistic and professional achievements.

Being an artist comes with many romantic notions and many of them are untrue. Many immature individuals who choose to become artists often escape from reality and see the artist's life through rose-colored glasses. They often abuse drugs, alcohol and sex. They may refuse to get a job and live the life of the romantic gypsy. They may believe their fellow classmates from art school who are now earning an income from their art have "sold out."

One of the greatest misconceptions young artists have is all they have to do is create art and an agent or gallery will take care of all of the business responsibilities. In truth, any agent or dealer who is worth their weight prefers to represent an artist who has achieved career and financial maturity and who understands the business of art from their point of view and applies the tools to elevate their career. A few years ago when I moderated a panel discussion with New York City dealers at the Atlantic Gallery I asked: "Should an artist have a track record before they approach you?" Laurie de Chiara said, "I want to know that an artist is having a continuum in their career." James Cavello, owner of the Westwood Gallery replied, "It is important that an artist understand at all times that their dealer is their partner. We're working together to achieve one goal and that goal is to sell that work of art."

The fact that you are reading this book indicates you are a proactive artist and most likely not a Sleeping Beauty. However, if you know any artist who fits the description you may want to say to them: "Wake up and smell the coffee!" Then, share some advice with them, such as hire the best representatives they can – themselves – and set goals to improve self-sufficiency. (You may also want to give them a copy of this book as a gift.)

TAME THE CREATIVE BEAST

In your life time you can do anything you want,
you just won't have time to do everything you want.

Creative success depends on nurturing "The Inner Child," but when "The Inner Child" is not tempered by reason and logic it may swell into "The Creative Beast" and attack other areas of our lives. Jack is an exciting, creative person whose inner child often takes control over his adult life. I endearingly refer to him as "Jack The Juggler" because he is a teacher, painter and photographer. He is trying to write a book and may return to school to get a degree in art therapy. His crowded apartment is cluttered with many unfinished projects. Without any concrete plan he is juggling so many balls in the air they are crashing down around him in a life of chaos, stress, indecision and unfulfilled dreams.

Jack needs to tame "The Creative Beast." If he focused on pursuing one goal and brought it to fruition, he would enjoy the challenge, diversity and rewards that come from commitment, discipline and experience. He would attain success and peace of mind. Achieving excellence and recognition in one area would help him achieve other goals with equal success.

If "The Creative Beast" ever causes your life to spin out of control get it back into control by exercising parental supervision and patience. Realize there are only twenty-four hours in a day. *(Refer to the chapters Create Your Master Plan & Plan Your Destiny and do the exercises.)* Stay committed to your life's mission. Consider seeing a career coach to help you clarify and focus on your goals as well as help you attain organization and direction.

AVOID STRIVING FOR PERFECTION

Have no fear of perfection – you'll never reach it.
Salvador Dali

Perfectionism is a self-sabotaging activity that invites the critic and the judge to enter your sacred realm and sit on each of your shoulders, dictating your every move. It is healthier to aim toward excellence than perfectionism, otherwise you will be in torment every time you stumble and stub your toe. Dismiss the extreme notion of success and failure. Works of art never fail and you are never a failure. A project may not come out as you expected, but its value may be more than what you first see. Instead of calling them "mistakes" – a word that will only perpetuate discouragement – call them "opportunities to learn." Thomas A. Edison denied that he had made 10,000 mistakes when trying to design the light bulb. Instead he said that he had learned 10,000 ways *not* to do it. The inventor of self-stick notes was trying to invent a form of glue when a "mistake" occurred. What a brilliant "mistake" that was!

We live in an imperfect world. Instead of allowing the flaws lead to frustration embrace them. The performance in which you forget your lines may help you become a better improviser. The can of paint that spills on your canvas may help you loosen up your style. The paper that gets chewed in the etching press, the marble that shatters under your chisel or the pages of poetry that are lost due to a computer virus are gifts that teach us to be tolerant and accepting of the real world and yourself.

Julia Soul said: "If you are never scared, embarrassed or hurt, it means you never take chances." If the fear of failure is preventing you from making a sincere effort, remember one thing all successful people have in common is that they have all tried and failed many times along the road to success.

Be patient and consistent in your efforts, and don't expect immediate results. Enjoy the journey. Your life is more than setting and attaining goals. The rewards are derived from the kind of person you grow into during your process.

Life's a banquet, and most poor suckers are starving to death.
Auntie Mame

Ann achieved her long awaited dream of being the producer of her first event. She jumped into the project head first. As she faced new challenges she called me almost every week and grumbled about the problems she was facing, which included friction among the artists and crewmembers, flaws in the production and delays in receiving payment. Most of her grievances were minor, often exaggerated and were easily corrected with the practical solutions I offered. The attention she was giving to the "small stuff" was stealing her vitality and productivity.

During one of her phone calls I stopped her in the middle of a sentence and said, "Ann, celebrate! Be proud of yourself for having the talent, courage and determination to bring a creative concept to fruition! Focus on how wonderful you will feel at the opening!" She became speechless for a moment and then giggled with delight. She suddenly began to see the larger picture. She was in the process of one of the most challenging and rewarding times of her life and had forgotten to rejoice. From that day forward she discovered new tools to finish the project with renewed energy, a positive attitude and ahead of schedule.

CHAPTER 5

TAKING CARE OF BUSINESS

THE ROLE OF THE ARTREPRENEUR

As the old saying goes,
good work, good pay.
Giotto

In addition to creating the art, the artist who wants to earn a living is required to navigate through a complex terrain of administrative tasks, marketing strategies, negotiations and technical applications. Unfortunately, in today's world, many talented artists flounder because they fail to develop even the smallest amount of business acumen.

Taking care of business means planning for success. If you decide to take your art beyond the hobby stages, then you will have to deal with business. In the dictionary you will find an "entrepreneur" as "One who owns, launches, manages and assumes the risk of an economic venture." The successful artist of the new millennium is what I call an Artrepreneur, a rare combination of creative artist and responsible businessperson. Each artist has to find his or her own balance between creative satisfaction and financial security.

In a workshop, while I was discussing "The Role of the Artrepreneur" a woman in the first row yelled out to me: "How can you expect the artist to do everything? Isn't it enough that we make the art? It's not fair!" In response to this sudden outburst, I heard many chuckles from other students and I saw several heads nod in agreement. Her response was honest. When the artist makes the decision to try to live off their art difficult decisions and sacrifices go with the territory. Being an artist isn't always as romantic as we wish. There are pressures to produce the art, seek exhibition venues and take care of mundane details – even after you have attained prominence. Sculptor Bruce Beasley, whose work is in the permanent collection of the Museum of Modern Art and the Guggenheim, said in the book *The Business of Art* by Lee Caplin: "If I'm going to live off my work, I must pay more attention to the business part than if I had another source of income. It is like sweeping up the studio or changing the oil in the air compressor; it isn't interesting or aesthetic, but it is a reality that has to be dealt with."

Whether we like it or not artists have to take care of business. During the past two decades, positive changes have increased their power and made it easier. After the art boom in the '80's, many art buyers lost faith in the dealers that misdirected them, and they have become more educated consumers, seeking out artists directly. The Internet has provided a growing intimacy between the artist and the art buyer. Books on the business of art are available to educate artists. Many career advisors, like myself, are counseling and presenting seminars on business issues. A growing number of artists are advertising in art magazines with their studio addresses and telephone numbers and their own web sites. Many artists are curating their own exhibitions and establishing their own galleries. And, artists everywhere are virtually transforming corporate spaces, parks, restaurants, bookstores and a range of other public and private spaces as exhibition venues.

> *What lies behind us and what lies before us*
> *are tiny matters compared to what lies within us.*
> Ralph Waldo Emerson

THE RULE OF THIRDS

CREATOR, MANAGER AND ADMINISTRATOR

As an Artrepreneur you will essentially have three roles: creator of the art; manager of marketing and promotion; and administrator. These three essential roles will not always be equally divided but if you want your career to soar try at first for hour you spend creating art, spend one hour managing your career and another caring for the administrative tasks – much of which can be delegated – to earn more time for creativity.

Lisa was determined to become a full-time artist and had accumulated a large inventory of paintings in three years. Her work depicted Native American history based on old murals on edifices that were about to be destroyed and replaced by luxury buildings. She had very little business and administrative experience but she had a solid, inspiring body of work with human-interest value. I suggested that she spend the next few months focusing on the marketing phase of her career, which meant sacrificing some studio time. Lisa realized the effort required to attain her financial goals would be worth the short-term sacrifice.

To have ideas is to gather flowers.
To think is to weave them into garlands.
Anne-Sophie Swetchine

First we determined her budget and made an itemized list of expenses. Then we compiled a database of appropriate market leads, consisting of organizations, galleries, institutions, cultural groups, libraries, museums, private individuals and corporations that would be interested in her work. In addition to galleries and museums our list included writers, publications, news directors and station managers, who would be interested in the story behind her work. We then created a small brochure and wrote cover letters and press releases that explained the significance of her project. We separated our prospects into two lists – hot (those we knew) and cold (those we didn't know.) We began with the "Hot List" first and made phone calls before mailing the brochure to find out if they wanted more materials. She recruited some volunteers among her family members and friends.

Armed with a financial plan, a targeted market, and a large dose of persistence, in about four months Lisa acquired three gallery exhibitions, one museum exhibition, five sales and several commissions. As a result of the publicity efforts, she was profiled in several local and national publications and on the TV news.

In Lisa's situation, "The Rule of Thirds" consisted of three years as the creator and only four months working as the manager and administrator. She earned the freedom to return to her studio full time and had the resources to hire an assistant to handle the administrative details and some of the manager's duties.

I am opposed to millionaires,
but it would be dangerous to offer me the position.

Mark Twain

BUSINESS TOOLS: A CHECKLIST

To become a successful Artrepreneur you will need some business tools such as:

- Business Name
- Business Type such as: Self-employed, Corporation, Partnership, limited partnership, non-profit corporation
- Business License
- Checking Account
- Receipts
- Sales Tax Permit
- Insurance
- Phone and Answering Machine / Service
- Fax machine
- Computer

- Mailing List
- Rolodex
- File folders and cabinet
- Letterhead
- Logo
- Envelopes
- Postage
- Shipping Boxes
- Packing Tape
- Calendar
- Appointment Book
- Pens and pencils
- Pencil Sharpener
- Art Resource books

FORECASTING YOUR CASH FLOW

Many artists have no idea whether or not they are making any money, where their customers are coming from, and whether their profits are going up or down. They have no control over their finances. As an Artrepreneur every aspect of your business, every choice you make, is either earning money or costing you money. Your business expenses, projected income, profits and losses, cannot be ignored. Most business people fail because they ignore their cash flow. Keeping financial records and understanding them is vital. When you take control over your cash flow you become more powerful in other areas of your career.

"What is cash flow?" If you look at your projected income or revenue, then compare it with all the expenditures you need to keep the business running, the difference is your cash flow. Metaphorically speaking, like water cash sometimes flows abundantly to you, and sometimes it seems to evaporate. You don't want to be adrift at sea without financial security during the unexpected turbulent times. To keep the tides running in your favor, and prepare for rainy days, you need to do cash forecasting.

To forecast your cash flow future, take a look at your financial history. Review your records of sales and expenses for up to the last three to five years. You'll be able to determine in which months you had the highest cash flow, and which months you had the lowest cash flow. Now, do the same for your expenses. Compare the two. After examining your cash flow over a period of time, you will notice the emergence of definite financial patterns.

When you discover those high and low periods in your business, you can make necessary contingency plans. You will want to pay particular attention to those periods in which your expenses are high and your cash flow is low. Without a plan to increase income and decrease expenses, you will run into trouble that could have been avoided. This trouble will be worsened by outside factors that you cannot control such as economic decline, health problems, medical expenses or your gallery's bankruptcy.

Compare your budgeted and actual figures to learn where costs are going. Keep a detailed journal of your expenses to determine where you can trim costs and determine unnecessary expenses are draining your profit.

Time is money, and if you eliminate the ways you waste time you will save money. Don't hesitate to spend money in areas that will help you gain time and attain efficiency. One example is to purchase office equipment such as a computer, especially now that they are so affordable and user-friendly. A computer will help you maintain your financial records, mailing list, résumé and business correspondence. It will also help you obtain vital information from the Internet. *(See the section Managing Your Time and 17 Time-Saving Strategies in this chapter.)*

There are many helpful books and soft ware programs that will help you to manage your money. *Working Solo: The Real Guide to Freedom and Financial Success with Your Own Business*, by Terri Lonier and *Small Business for Dummies* by Eric Tyson and Jim Schell are two of many helpful books available. *(See Appendix II.)*

YOUR BUSINESS PLAN

A written business plan will consist of a plan of action. It will show any prospective investors or bankers that you are serious about earning a profit from your art. Perhaps the greatest benefit for the business plan, however, is it will force you to create a clear path to take your art career and avoid leaving it to chance. Your business plan will require updating so once you create it don't neglect it.

The business plan consists of four parts: business statement; production plan; financial plan and marketing plan.
- The business statement describes your business goals. It includes what you plan to sell and any additional sources of income such as private teaching and merchandising.

- The production plan describes how you plan to produce the art, how long it will take, plus required facilities, equipment, art supplies and hired help. Add office equipment, supplies and business services, such as legal and accounting fees.
- The financial plan indicates the amount of money you expect to earn and the amount needed to begin or expand your business. As a rule, your operating expenses should be less than twenty percent of your income. That should be your ideal goal.
- The marketing plan describes your market, your customers and your competition. It explains the unique features of your art or art service and benefits to the buyer. It includes where you plan to advertise, what marketing materials you will generate to reach your prospective buyers, and investments you will make to expand your markets. *(Refer to the chapters Create Your Master Plan & Plan Your Destiny and Finding Your Buyers & Building Your Markets.)*

Business without profit is not business
any more than a pickle is candy.
Charles F. Abbott

PRICING YOUR WORK

I have curated more than fifty exhibitions and have learned that most emerging artists are clueless about pricing their work. Your prices should be competitive in the marketplace, not a number you pick out of the air. When determining your prices, be realistic. Has your work passed the test of selling to several art buyers outside your coterie of friends and relatives? Although relatives and friends might be staunch admirers of your work they may not be qualified to determine your prices. Collect a consensus of opinion from professionals in the field. Make some important decisions, such as: To whom do you want to sell your work? Do you wish to price your work high and be satisfied with a few, infrequent sales, or would you rather price your work fairly and raise the prices as the value of your work increases? It's easier to raise prices than lower them and it's the selling price that matters, not the asking price.

To price your work properly it is important to keep time and expense records of direct and indirect costs. Direct costs include things like the number of hours you spent on the work, including developing the concept and preliminary sketches, plus the expenses for materials, and your labor costs. Set your labor costs by deciding what you want to earn yearly and divide by the number of hours you work. Indirect costs include such items as rent, utilities, insurance, advertising, shipping and printing. Add these costs and divide by the number of hours you work each year. For example, if you spent $5,000 this past year on expenses and worked 1,000 hours creating art your costs are $5 per hour. Add that to your desired hour rate (for example $25) and your total is $30 per hour. If it takes ten hours to complete a work your total indirect costs for that work would be $300. If you create ten works a year you would need to earn $3,000 to break even. After you tabulate your costs and profit you can regulate your prices by setting a figure by the square inch or square foot.

PRICING STRATEGIES

- **Research the market.** Go to galleries, art fairs and auctions. Do a comparative study between your work and others in the same style, media, subject matter, complexity and detail, technical ability, professional experience, education and talent. Collect résumés, brochures and price lists.

- **Compare prices with selling artists.** Don't use vanity galleries or artists who are not selling as comparative standards.
- **Beware of sales tactics.** Look for inconsistencies. Original works are sometimes set at a high price as a maneuver to increase the sales of the artist's limited editions.
- **Timing is important.** If you are considering selling in a gallery, consider your loss of profit after the gallery takes a commission. Selling in a gallery has its rewards, but you might be better waiting for your work to increase in value.
- **Establish a market for your work.** Don't wait too long to exhibit or you might find yourself with a large inventory and no buyers on your mailing list. Build sales by exhibiting in alternative spaces and beginner galleries.
- **Get it in writing.** When a gallery offers to sell your work get a written agreement of the retail price. This way you gain control of your prices rather than offering them a wholesale price, which they can mark up as high as they choose.
- **Add value to your work.** Strive for excellence and develop your own trademark style. Strengthen your position and build your credentials through winning awards, getting publicity, having one-person shows and increasing sales.
- **Present your work properly.** Look for ways to improve the quality of your presentation such as upgrading your framing or using archival materials.
- **Don't sell your work at wholesale prices.** Avoid the reputation of offering "bargain" prices in your studio while your gallery is charging retail. Your reputation will suffer and you will risk losing the gallery.
- **Keep your prices consistent.** Whether your buyers are in New York or Chicago they should pay the same price.

A thing is worth
Whatever the buyer will pay for it.
Publilius Syrus

- **Don't price your work emotionally.** If you are attached to a piece instead of fixing an excessively high price on it mark it "sold" or "in the artist's collection."
- **Know when to offer discounts.** Museums often receive a discounts and it is justified by the fact that the sale will likely boost your reputation. Discounts are also given to buyers who buy several works at once or within a short time period.
- **Know when to raise prices.** The time to raise your prices is when you've established a proven track record of sales and the demand for your work is consistently high for at least a year. Experts say when you're selling at least half of everything you produce within a six-month time period you can increase prices 10-25% each year.
- **Adjust to the changing economy.** If there is interest in your work but it hasn't sold for several months offer installment plans, introduce smaller works, change to a less costly medium or create prints until the economy improves. If selling your art is your only source of income try teaching, lecturing or taking on commissions.
- **Be prepared for success.** As you grow so will your buyers. When the value of your work increases you may be able to educate your existing buyers to pay more, but don't be disappointed if you lose some of them. If so, replace them by altering your marketing plan and exhibition venues. You may need to move your work galleries that attract a higher clientele.

MANAGING YOUR TIME

Time often appears as our rival in the game of life as we try to control it, get ahead of it and make the most of it. We juggle several balls at once – raising children, caring for elderly parents, having a job and creating art. It is no surprise that stress is the buzzword of our time, with a plethora of medication and homeopathic remedies on the market. We need help!

We all waste time unintentionally. Among the top time wasters are: telephone socializing, junk mail, a poorly organized work area, lack of essential information, excessive red tape and paperwork, poorly planned procedures, failure to plan and implement priorities, poor skills in delegating, training and conceptualizing, procrastinating, poor scheduling, over-committing, attempting to do too much at once, and striving for perfection.

Creativity has its own force that refuses to abide by logic, organization and discipline. It is easy to become immersed in the creative process and let time disappear into thin air. To be a successful Artrepreneur we need to manage time efficiently. If we want to decrease the stress in our lives we need to employ some time management tools.

17 TIME-SAVING STRATEGIES

- **Be committed to the project at hand.** Set aside sufficient time without any distractions. Rehearse the task mentally. Quiet the mind. Focus your attention. Take each step deliberately. Become totally absorbed in what you're doing, and a free-flowing momentum will transpire.

- **Use modern technology to improve efficiency.** Answering machines, fax machines, computers, copy machines, scanners and digital cameras are user-friendly and very affordable. Multi-purpose machines combine fax, phone and printer and save desk space and hours of manual labor.

- **Plan ahead.** Incorporate your career plans into your daily routine. Make and use lists, calendars and appointment books. Alphabetize your files and organize your materials to help you locate them quickly.

- **Add pleasure to your tasks.** Buy and/or create such materials that are colorful, well designed and aesthetically appealing to you to make working with them a creative experience.

- **Create an uncluttered work area.** It should be free from visual and sound distractions. If possible use a separate room for an office or arrange a space in a corner of your studio, bedroom or a closet. In this work area place your phone, rolodex, appointment book and a file cabinet to store your photographs, slide sheets, résumé and business receipts.

- **Be prepared.** Make tomorrow's plans and write your "To Do" list the night before and arrange the activities in order of urgency. Create promotional materials by the dozens and have several sets of slides on file. Keep several copies of your current résumé ready to go. Maintain your mailing list on the computer and keep it up to date.

To nurture your creative aspect,
you must put a hermetically sealed retort,
so that there is no intrusion,
around a certain number of hours each day...
and that time must be inviolate.
Joseph Campbell

- **Keep a closed door to your private studio.** This should be your sacred space. Let others know that you want to be left alone with your creativity. You should also provide time to brainstorm, daydream, meditate and restore balance. Set limits on your social and family demands.
- **Break large projects down into smaller chunks**. If you are setting aside important projects waiting for that big block of time to be available you'll discover that it may never arrive. It is better to use the five-minute strategy and tackle the project with small amounts of time on a regular basis.
- **Practice discipline.** One of the hardest aspects of a small business or home-based business is creating the discipline or motivation to work each day.
- **Set aside time each day and/or week to work on your career.** Ideally, this should be a peak energy time when you have the ability to focus and concentrate on details.
- **Discover your time-wasting habits.** List every activity and the time it took, including distractions such as useless phone chatter and looking for papers that have not been filed away properly. Periodically, ask yourself whether the task you're doing is urgent or important. If neither, move on to something else that is.
- **Ask for help.** When we are reluctant to ask for help we end up wasting time, becoming frustrated or making costly mistakes. Hire a professional specialist when needed.

- **Delegate simple tasks.** High school or college interns or retirees can help you do research on the Internet, stretch canvases, prepare mailings, send e-mails and type letters.
- **Become a master at slowing time.** Pay attention to the small miracles of life. Reconnect with a sense of discovery and try to see events unfold through the eyes of a child, watching the first sunrise, or the miraculous way birds fly together in formations. Find a way to meditate. This tip alone will reduce your stress level and help you become more productive.
- **Dismiss all the reoccurring irritations and annoyances.** When you come across a problem, don't just fix it for now, get to the root of it and re-design your behavior. For example, if you are spending too much time taking personal phone calls, either put a time limit on them or get an answering machine or Caller ID to monitor them.
- **Avoid procrastination.** This is one of the major causes of failure. The pain of trying to finish a project at the last hour is greater than confronting it immediately. Some of the reasons for procrastination are: fear of failure; fear of success; fear of change; fear of the unknown; fear of responsibilities; lack of motivation; lack of skill and lack of preparation. If you procrastinate excessively consider hiring a career coach.
- **Finish dreaded tasks first.** Most of us postpone a project we dislike, only to have it hang over our heads worrying about it, feeling guilty about not doing it, and finding excuses not to do it. If you just do it, you will feel a sense of relief. Often, the dreaded tasks are not as undesirable as we thought and might bring positive results. After you finish a dreaded task, reward yourself with a favorite activity or treat.
- **Maintain good health.** In the battle against time and aging, you cannot ignore the correlation between good nutrition,

mental and spiritual health, and the avoidance of disease. If your health is impaired, your career will be threatened. Exercise regularly. Avoid the use of toxic artist materials, as well as toxic environments and relationships. You may frequently be tempted to work long and hard in your studio and neglect your nutritional needs. Have plenty of healthy snacks, fresh fruits and vegetables and clean drinking water close at hand.

"Do not go where the path may lead,
go instead where there is no path and leave a trail."
Ralph Waldo Emerson

INCREASE YOUR INCOME WITHOUT HAVING TO WORK NINE TO FIVE

You may not always be able to earn sufficient income from the sale of your work. Depending on a range of factors including your risk tolerance, skills, responsibilities and personality there are a range of career options available. At times you can take a job outside the art profession: Kandinsky taught law; Gauguin was a stockbroker; Alex Katz painted houses; Julian Schnabel drove a cab. However, if you're like many artists and abhor the mundane and routine of normal working environments, you'll be pleased to know that many artists have turned creativity into cash by thinking outside the cubicle.

When I was an aspiring artist in order to avoid having to "go to work" I strove very hard to maintain my freedom. I rented a studio and sold other artists' work plus my own. At times I gave private art lessons and sold art supplies. I designed a line of hand-painted apparel and sold it through my studio and several boutiques. Making a living was an act of creating balance. It was not easy or profitable in the beginning but I developed determination, discipline, and a hard work ethic – all attributes that I carried with me as my profession evolved. I have been self-supporting ever since.

ARTREPRENEURS WHO CREATE INCOME

- Susan, a graphic designer and painter, helps other artists with the designing of their promotional materials. Her part-time service brings in a few thousand dollars each month.
- Raúl, a printmaker, disliked paying an artist to print his etchings. When an affordable etching press became available he borrowed money from his father, provided printmaking services to fellow artists and in less than six months he paid back the loan and increased the profits on his own work.
- Lee has a degree in Art History and enjoys escorting her non-artist friends to museums and galleries. Upon a friend's suggestion she contacted the continuing education department of a nearby college and offered a lecture tour for neophyte art lovers. It caught on and in a short time she developed a loyal following and a big supplementary income.
- Joan is a painter known for her expressive use of color. With a degree in psychology she fused her knowledge of art with the psychology of color and transformed it into cash by becoming a color consultant and lecturer. Known as a color expert she now commands more money for her paintings.
- Vassilios, an artist and owner of an SUV knows that shipping art can be expensive and risky for artists so he started a part-time, lucrative transporting business that involves packing the work and delivering it to the exhibition.

- Gerda has an educational background in fine art and web site design. She volunteered to design the web site for her art organization. When each member wanted their own individual web site they hired her. Her business has blossomed and she now has a graphic design student to assist her, which affords her more time to create her fine art.

- Barbara enjoys studying esoteric subjects and has acquired proficient knowledge in *feng shui* (an ancient practice that helps to balance the energy flow in our environment). Her work combines those elements. In her business she advises her clients on the best art to purchase according to the *feng shui* principles and creates art on commission to suit them.

- Dana has created hundreds of drawings inspired by quotes of famous people over the ages. While browsing in a bookstore an idea came to her to create a series of books using her images accompanied by the quotations. She started a self-publishing company using digital printing on demand and autographs, numbers and sells limited edition books in fairs and on the Internet.

- Ben found it easier and more fun to sell the work of fellow members of his cooperative gallery than to sell his own. He charges an hourly fee to sit in the gallery plus a small sales commission. The artists gladly pay him to converse with the visitors, sell the work and keep detailed records.

- Sonja quit her secretarial job to devote more time to creating art. To augment her income she became an agent for hire. She provides administrative services for artists who have a disdain for the tedium of business.

How can you turn your unique skills into income?

Chapter 6

Relationships: Building Your Power Base

We must, indeed, all hang together,
or most assuredly we will all hang separately.
Benjamin Franklin

As in any other career field an artist can either rise to fame or fall to anonymity depending upon with whom he or she associates. The single most valuable part of your career may be the relationships you develop. When you think of key events in your professional life that marked a turning point such as having your first exhibition or appearing in the newspaper most likely it would not have occurred without the help of a friend, agent, artist, gallery owner, art buyer, writer or juror making a decision or taking an action that changed the course of your career.

In today's professional world, building strong relationships is a survival skill that provides stability and insurance. In the highly competitive artistic community, much of your success relies on the support and camaraderie of fellow artists, art writers and critics, grant givers, dealers, collectors and other individuals.

You need allies. We know that Mary Cassatt spent most of her life in France and was allied herself with the impressionists Manet and Degas early in her career. Jean Arp could not have prospered without his connection with the Blaue Reiter in Munich and various avant-garde groups in Paris, including the surrealists, and the Dadaists in Zürich.

Collectors recommend artists to dealers. Galleries seek the advice of the artists they represent when adding new artists. Many grant givers require endorsements from art leaders. Art writers obtain story ideas from other art professionals. Simply, the more people who know about you, your talent and your abilities – especially the leaders in your field – the greater chance you'll have of attracting the opportunities, jobs, resources, money and prestige that you want.

As they say, it's a small world. The more time you spend in your art community, you will notice that it actually consists of a relatively small group of people who play musical chairs. The division among art careers used to be much more defined. In recent years, however, the roles of artists, art dealers, critics and collectors have become interchangeable. The artist is often a curator, the collector has become a consultant and the art dealer may have many roles. It is wise to cultivate strong ties with those people who are committed to being involved in the art world for the long haul. And since that is not always obvious, you shouldn't burn any bridges along the way.

In creating our book *The Complete Guide to New York Art Galleries*, we asked every dealer about their selection process and offered these choices: How many artists do you select from professional referrals? How many artists are selected from slides and other materials you receive? How many artists are selected from seeing their work in exhibitions and artists' studios? Many galleries state that most of the artists are selected from professional referrals. Although galleries often discover artists from unsolicited materials sent through the mail, an introduction to the gallery by a mutual friend or professional associate will increase your chances. Knowing well-positioned professionals will not guarantee success, but the doors will often open quicker. Once you step inside, it's up to you.

In *The Business of Art* author Lee Caplin says, "There is no evidence that socializing with museum people is of direct assistance in the system of showing contemporary art, but there is no evidence that it has hurt too many artists." He continues to say, "If the result is not useful for exhibitions, you still might develop some friendships, or at least a better mutual understanding of the world of the artist and the world of the museum-worker."

Selection process: 75% of the artists are selected from professional referrals; 20% from slides sent to the gallery; and 5% from art seen in exhibitions or artists' studios.
Denise Bibro

The act of building relationships offers a wealth of opportunities and the opportunities. It is an activity that takes place everywhere with everyone. Some of the most productive contacts come from chance encounters – waiting for the bus or in the grocery check-out line, in the doctor's waiting room or at the post office, at a place of worship or at your child's school.

Proactive artists don't wait for chance encounters. Whenever they attend an event their antenna is up in order to meet the most important people in the room. An artist who is focused on climbing the ladder knows the importance of building their reputation by developing a spirit of cooperation with others.

Opportunities multiply as they are seized.
SunTzu

To succeed at networking it helps to remember these basic principles: **Hunt** (seek out relationships); **Farm** (cultivate relationships) and **Feed** (nourish your relationships).

A good "hunter" is always searching for new contacts and alliances wherever they go. They establish relationships as a result of searching for mutual benefits. A good "farmer" is a good listener, accepts other people's differences in opinions, and is non-judgmental. He or she is able to interact with different types of people. A good "feeder" invests time and effort in sharing and nurturing relationships. They know how to follow up.

Enrich your relationships by becoming a good matchmaker. Bringing people together is one of the strongest links in my career success. It is very exciting when my introductions lead to professional alliances and friendships. I've learned that intimate cocktail receptions in my apartment are more resourceful than large-scale events. I encourage you to develop your own system of hosting and matchmaking. It's contagious!

Relationship building is a reciprocal process. It works best with the attitude that it is as rewarding to give information, services, resources, advice and referrals as it is to receive. Give to others with a spirit of generosity. When you have an opportunity to provide something, give much more than is requested – go far beyond the recipient's expectations. This practice will reward you with a reputation for being someone others can count on more than others.

When I give a lecture I always arrive early to meet each attendee personally. I provide many free handouts and many more ideas, facts, resources and strategies than what is anticipated. I also encourage the attendees to network with each other to create a relaxed sense of camaraderie. The sponsors and attendees of my lectures are extremely grateful that I go beyond their expectations. They respond with glowing testimonials and referrals.

Dismiss any fear of being robbed of your creativity and share it willingly. Share your art, resources and your ideas, not only with artists, but also with other professionals, organizations and communities. Those who have great wisdom have said you only really own what you give away.

STRATEGIES FOR BUILDING RELATIONSHIPS

- **Be prepared to meet new people.** Carry an ample supply of visual "handouts" – postcards, business cards or brochures – that that feature an image of your work. Keep them in a clean, protective case. I have two card cases – one in my briefcase and another in my handbag. When I go to an event I also place some extra cards in my pocket for quick access.
- **Keep records.** After you exchange cards with someone, jot down a reminder on the back of that person's card such as where you met, what you discussed and how and when you should follow up. Record new acquaintances and contacts in a rolodex, computer file or index cards. Set up whatever system works best for you.
- **Be polite.** This sounds obvious but is often forgotten. Simple acts of etiquette go a long way in your favor. Use every op-

portunity to send a personal note or e-mail to say "thank you," "congratulations" or "it was a pleasure to meet you."

- **Serve the art community.** There are many activities to choose from such as curating, jurying or lecturing.
- **Write about art.** If you enjoy covering the art scene offer to write a column for your local community newspaper. Several artists have served on the editorial board of *Manhattan Arts International* E-zine. As members of the press they interview leaders in the art field and are invited to special press events.
- **Become a host.** Offer to help at the information table or check in desk, at the next event you attend. Become the friendly greeter to those who feel uncomfortable in a crowd.
- **Use cyberspace.** Network through chat rooms and message boards.
- **Go where the action is.** Attend gallery receptions, lectures, symposiums and events held in museums and art centers. Visit the art expositions and galleries in major cities and talk to the salespeople and dealers.
- **Go to the top.** Offer to become an assistant for an established artist or take a job in a leading gallery.
- **Get involved.** Volunteer to work on the events or publicity committee of your art organization or for a favorite political candidate. As a committee chairperson organize lectures with leading curators, dealers and critics.
- **Extend an invitation.** Contact a famous artist you admire and ask to exchange studio visits.
- **Take one step forward each day.** Make at least one phone call that will widen your circle of connections.

How can you improve and increase the ways in which you hunt, farm and feed your relationships?

It is not so much our friends' help that helps us
as the confident knowledge that they will help us.
Epicurus

CAMARADERIE

Your rolodexes may be overflowing with contact names, but there is nothing more nurturing than establishing camaraderie with others. Camaraderie develops through mutual trust and shared missions. When such a bond is formed, it is deeply rewarding and empowering. Artists who feel isolated don't have to look far to find the real companionship they need is within the artist population. There is a staggering number of artists to join for solace and strength. According to U.S. government statistics found at www.bls.gov/home.htm about 149,000 artists held jobs in 2002. More than half were self-employed – about seven times the proportion in all professional and related occupations. The number is expected to increase 10-20% by the year 2012.

Unfortunately, many artists may not look upon their fellow artists as strong allies. They may argue that being an artist is a highly competitive profession; there are more artists than there are venues to accommodate them. However, there are limitless opportunities if you dare to find and create them. Artists who believe there is enough for everyone exude a spirit of cooperation and enthusiasm. They take an assertive approach to make changes in their careers and reach out to help other artists. They become curators, or organizers of community arts' projects, or launch a cooperative gallery. They often work tirelessly without pay or accolades in order to improve the status of all artists.

Donna Marxer, is such an artist. She is a recognized painter, writer, public speaker and arts activist. She was the Executive Director of Artists Talk On Art, a panel series in New York dedicated to addressing artists' concerns. She was a board member of New York's Organization of Independent Artists as well as Founder and Chairman of "Quarterly Report," a feminist roundtable. She also serves as a juror for national exhibitions and was recently a visual arts panelist for the Ohio State Arts Council. As a highly respected arts writer, Marxer is a regular columnist for *Art Calendar* magazine and has been a contributor to national art publications since the '60's. As a labor of love, she is contributor of a series of oral interviews with older women artists for the National Archives of American Art. She offers this sage advice: "First and foremost, artists should give up self-pity and do their work. Despair and fear of failure must be fought against as the enemies of creativity. Then, we artists should help one another, share information instead of hugging secrets. When we give out instead of hoarding our hurts, the pain becomes manageable and we are also doing some good for others."

Once you make a decision,
the universe conspires to make it happen.
Ralph Waldo Emerson

THE POWER OF ARTISTS' ORGANIZATIONS

Margaret Mead said, "Never doubt that a small group of thoughtful, committed individuals can change the world, indeed it's the only thing that ever has." That's how I feel about the importance of joining and supporting artists' organizations. Their value has increased since our society has become increasingly depersonalized. The artists' organization offers the artist a place to share values, convictions, ambitions and solutions to common problems. It empowers the artist-activist who wants to make positive changes. It offers camaraderie and a support system for creative, spiritual and political development. It is the quickest way for an artist to feel less like an outsider. It is one of the best routes for a beginning artist to develop an exhibition history.

An effective organization has a purpose that is shared by all its members and to which they will willingly commit their efforts. People working together can do almost anything.
James L. Hayes

There are regional, local, national and international groups in different sizes with different activities and missions. You can choose from a variety of artists' organizations, each one fulfilling a variety of different needs – for exhibitions, intellectual stimulation, political, social and professional activities or vital information on health, safety and legal issues. Some artists' organizations, like the American Watercolor Society, the National Sculpture Society and The Camera Club supply information about specific mediums and showcase artists working in that medium. Other organizations focus on business and economic changes in the world of art. Several national organizations offer discounts on insurance, rental cars, art books, art supplies and other business expenses. A number of organizations meet and present slide shows to critique each other's work and take trips to museums and artists' studios. Most organizations publish newsletters and have web sites that offer communication links and resources. A growing practice for organizations is to provide career and business guidance regarding self-promotion, marketing, portfolio presentation and pricing through panel discussions and workshops with guest professionals. Before selecting a group, visit their web sites, attend an event, read their newsletters, and speak to several different members to learn more about whether their benefits are suited to your needs.

Chicago Artists' Coalition in Chicago, IL, is a non-profit artists-run coalition of visual artists and friends to fulfill four basic needs: education of the general public regarding the value of the visual arts to society; advocacy of visual arts issues for members and the art community; professional and educational services for artists and the arts community; and improvement of the environment in which artists live and work.

Organization of Independent Artists (OIA) is an organization in New York City, which provides public spaces for exhibitions throughout the City. The gallery maintains a slide registry available to curators, art professionals, artists and others. OIA also publishes a newsletter and conducts slide viewings.

The West Side Arts Coalition is an organization with international members and its own exhibition space located in New York City. Artists join without being juried, however, some exhibitions are juried individually. The organization publishes a newsletter that highlights members' exhibitions and lists opportunities. The organization offers many other activities.

When you join an organization avoid being a passive member. Take a tip from John F. Kennedy and ask not what your organization can do for you, but what you can do for your organization. Volunteer to work on a committee or single project. You will not only be contributing to your organization you will be developing skills, knowledge and friendships not available elsewhere. For example, having a position on the publicity committee of your art organization will put you in direct contact with the press. If you volunteer to work on the events committee of your art organization, you can contact leading curators, dealers and critics to organize a panel discussion or series of lectures.

Regina Stewart is an artist and Executive Director of New York Artists Equity Association. The organization is an advocacy group that disseminates information regarding legislation and legal rights, all in the interest of effectively addressing "survival" issues relevant to artists. It has its own gallery, it publishes a journal and has a web site at www.anny.org. Regina offers this advice: "Join a nonprofit arts organization and help the greater community of artists. Volunteer to work on one of the organization's projects. Volunteering is personally and professionally rewarding. Your help benefits the organization and it enables you to meet not only other artists but the people who support and legislate the arts. New contacts and expanded knowledge are continuing sources of new and exciting options."

When you decide what is important to you, and there aren't any groups to fill your needs, consider starting your own. When I founded Artopia, the main purpose of the organization was to establish exhibition opportunities for its members. We also wanted to provide a forum where ideas could be exchanged, so in addition to the multi-media exhibitions, we held regular membership meetings and published a monthly newsletter. Realizing the importance of attracting support from the business community we offered a supporting membership category – lawyers, marketing professionals and members of the press – who shared their expertise with us and received discounts on members' artwork and invitations to our social events and private visits to artists' studios.

(See Appendix II for more artists' organizations.)

ADVICE FROM NANCY DI BENEDETTO
TO LEADERS OF ARTISTS ORGANIZATIONS

Nancy di Benedetto is a New York-based art and architecture historian, lecturer, curator, juror and consultant. She is a graduate of Yale with degrees in art history and English. She is a lecturer at the Metropolitan Museum of Art, New York School of Interior Design, Montclair Art Museum, English-Speaking Union and Marymount Manhattan College. She is the author of History of American Art *published by the Bridgewater Press and a consultant to numerous national arts organizations.*

Money, business and organization might sound like "dirty" words for the artist, but they are essential for a non-profit arts organization to thrive professionally and to survive financially. Here are some basic guidelines:

- Define clearly and succinctly a mission statement for yourselves as well as for the public. Who are you? What services do you provide that are unique?

- Hire a graphic designer to create a distinctive logo that is clearly recognizable. Use it consistently in all promotional material. It will project a solid, viable image.

- Provide a permanent administrative structure no matter how small the organization. A solely volunteer-run group is rudderless and will make it impossible to raise funding. Funders want to know *where* the money is going, *who* will be handling it and, most important, *how* it will be used.

- Establish a Board of Directors for guidance and money. It should consist primarily (three quarters) of people from the business world and the remaining one-quarter of well-known artists plus the Executive Director. They should be expected to make a sizeable financial contribution in order to join the board. This is an honor and they should be eager to support your cause. It should be an *active* board with rotating term limits.

- Select an Advisory Committee. This group should consist of established artists and/or prominent people in the field who will spread the word and assist you in fulfilling your goals. They usually do not require a monetary stipend.
- Locate a permanent gallery. Floating from one temporary space to another does not give a sense of permanence or stability.
- Develop fund raising ideas. There are many ways of raising money and giving the organization greater visibility and providing a financial cushion. This is a time-consuming endeavor but it is crucial for survival. Ideas are numerous, so this is the best test of creativeness.
- Even with limited resources these goals can be realized. With a strong organizational structure in place, a goal of running a successful business with the intent of developing a strong financial base, you are on the road to artistic success.

Without him I would have given up.
Pierre Auguste Renoir about Claude Monet

GETTING HELP FROM A CAREER CONSULTANT

There may be different stages of your career when you will want to acquire the services of a career consultant or career coach – to help you take your career to the next level. The services of a career consultant vary upon their skills, professional experience and geographic location. Since I started as a career consultant two decades ago most of the individuals who seek my advice want to leave their professions to become full-time artists. Their objects are to increase their income, achieve professional recognition and gain access to the New York City art community. In a career consultation, which consists of one or two hours either in person or on the phone I offer objective, constructive feedback on artwork and promotional materials. I help my clients clarify their financial, career and creative goals. I offer appropriate professional leads such as galleries, art writers and corporate art consultants. In essence, they receive a career road map, strategies and short and long term action steps.

When more intensive direction is required I expand my services to those of a career coach. In this capacity I provide the motivation, structure, direction, and on-going support to help my clients attain their career goals. We set up an advance series of telephone consultations to review progress and overcome roadblocks. Having a coach helps them stay on track, eliminate wasteful worry, and avoid procrastination.

An example of how I served as a career coach is when I helped Joanne plan her new business. We met twice a month for three months. I developed a business plan for her, which resulted in clarifying her objectives and getting financial backing from an investor. We worked on building her image and customer base. I introduced her work to individuals and companies that were appropriate for her and coached her on the best way to develop relationships with them.

Another example of how a career coach is invaluable to an artist is when a crisis occurs. Donna called me minutes after finishing a gallery presentation. She was devastated and felt her appointment went poorly. As she explained the situation I helped her separate the actual events from her interpretation. The appointment in reality went better than she thought. With some direction from me she proceeded to enhance her relationship with the dealer. I led her to a quick and positive resolution where she could be proactive. Needless to say, it saved her time and unnecessary anxiety.

Coaches are becoming one of the fastest growing service providers of this decade. There are over seventy coaching schools and coach training programs in the U.S. As in any profession not all consultants and coaches are alike. When seeking a good coach, look for someone who listens attentively, has compassion for your feelings, reserves judgment, and motivates you to take the best possible action to reach your most desired results. The best coach will have experience in business and the business of art, plus psychology and transformational work. A good coach will focus on helping you develop tools with which you can solve your problems by yourself, and will not try to make you depend upon him or her to solve them for you.

Let messengers and mentors give your dream wings. Build a support system in your work and in your personal life. If you cannot hire a professional career coach you can derive similar benefits through a mentor – a respected and trusted relative or friend, a member of the business community or an older artist. Choose one with whom you can meet or call on a routine basis to report progress and obtain sage advice. Seek out positive and motivational role models.

There may be critical times in your life when you need more than a mentor, career consultant or coach. You might find yourself overwhelmed by creative blocks, a fear of rejection, chronic frustration, depression or anxiety. Sandra Indig is a New York artist, arts therapist and analytic psychotherapist. She offers individual counseling for visual and performing artists, writers and poets. Among many things, she provides a safe, supportive atmosphere in which artists can explore issues, release blocked energy, bridge the gap between private space to public venue, and change habitual, unproductive behavior. She says, "I encourage the individual artist to face internal blocks which tend to inhibit full expression of his or her talent." She, and many other professionals in her field are offering a service of tremendous benefit for artists who need short-term therapy to help them through a critical time, or long-term assistance to resolve debilitating issues.

BUILD YOUR POWER BASE: AN EXERCISE

Build your power base by selecting the members of your professional team. Make a list of everyone you know and place them in two categories. A: Close contacts and B: Contacts you have through another person. List the professional benefits of having them on your team such as their specialized expertise, skill, product, information or service. Make a habit of reaching out to share and build your success with them!

_____

_____

_____

_____

_____

_____

_____

_____

_____

_____

_____

_____

Chapter 7

The Truth About (New York) Galleries

*Artists should have a credible representative
body of work before they submit their slides…
They should possess originality, a point of view,
command of technique and commitment.*
Heller Gallery

As a career consultant and the author of *The Complete Guide To New York Art Galleries* I am approached by artists from every corner of the globe to help them find a New York gallery. I wish I had a magic wand to match the perfect dealer to every artist I meet. The process of obtaining suitable representation is not easy. For more than seven years I have offered a course: "Artists: How to Sell Your Art" – also known as "How to Break into New York Galleries." In this three-hour, comprehensive seminar I try to de-mystify the gallery system. I strive to make sure that every artist acquires the inside knowledge, focus and fortitude to approach galleries. The course is offered each month, so I hope you will attend it.

Although this extensive chapter focuses on helping you understand how New York galleries generally operate the information can be applied to approaching dealers in any major city.

To help artists in their search for appropriate galleries, since 1995, my editorial assistants and I have produced and updated a comprehensive resource book titled *The Complete Guide To New York Art Galleries*. The galleries do not pay to be included, and that makes it an honest and comprehensive survey. We also contact each owner and director directly to obtain the information first hand. Matthew Deleget, Program Officer of New York Foundation for the Arts described it as "the only comprehensive source of its kind." This book has been referred to as everything from "the bible of the industry" to "manna from heaven."

We offer readers – artists as well as collectors – as much information as possible to help them make the right choice. To save artists time and energy we collect data from every dealer using a 40-question questionnaire. The profile includes contact names, address, telephone, fax and web site, owner's professional background, year the gallery was established, hours of operation, gallery size, focus and range of styles and media shown, mission or philosophy, number and origins of artists represented, a selection of artists and a description of their work, price ranges, market concentration (individual, corporate, museum or all three), the number of annual solo and group exhibitions, the publications in which the galleries advertise, their procedures for selecting artists, how and when artists, curators and organizations should approach the gallery, what materials they should send plus any special requirements, exhibition fees, membership dues, artists' stipends and additional information or services the gallery offers. Each listing has key words in the heading which informs the reader at first glance what the gallery's primary focus is such as "Contemporary / All Media" or "Private Dealer / Photography."

In the current edition of *The Complete Guide To New York Art Galleries* there are more than 1,000 galleries and alternative exhibition spaces, and many of them are accessible to under-recognized artists. This city attracts, influences, exhibits and sells artwork by artists from all continents in staggering numbers, thereby enhancing its multi-cultural vitality. In tiny rooms and giant lofts we find a colorful compendium of art movements and techniques, and every-visual-thing from Traditional to New Media, Outsider to Conceptual, Self-Taught to Site-Specific, Latin-American to Russian, Vintage to Video and Minimal to Pop. The terrain is vast and versatile, as well as complex and sometimes overwhelming – not only to outsiders, but also to the artists who live right in the midst of its ever-changing scenery.

From our years of experience interviewing gallery owners for this book and for our magazine *Manhattan Arts International* we learned there are many different dealers with different tastes, personalities and educational and cultural backgrounds. We also learned that dealers face numerous challenges dealers in operating a gallery including high real estate costs. When an unknown artist who has sold only a few pieces, approaches a gallery for an exhibition, he or she may not take into consideration the gallery's overhead and the high level of risk the gallery owner must take. For an artist to succeed, the gallery must invest time and money in promoting and marketing the artist's work. This commitment is not only based on the quality of the art, but also the work's marketing potential to the collectors that come to them for their guidance. Ivan Karp, owner of O.K. Harris Works of Art speaks for most serious collectors when he says in *The Business of Art* by Lee Caplin, "For the most part they look for sound track records and established names."

GETTING STARTED

Many opportunities exist for the artist who wants to break into the New York gallery system. New artists can take advantage of the plethora of alternative exhibition spaces and the non-profit venues that are mission-driven. They showcase new talent and many dealers discover artists in them. In New York's cultural centers, universities and government-funded art institutions artists obtain exposure, reviews and awards. Synagogue For The Arts' mission is: "To be an alternative space and exhibit a diversity of work and styles of emerging and established artists in a multi-purposed community setting." Marymount Manhattan College's exhibition program is: "To show the work of emerging artists who are not receiving enough exposure in commercial venues." Grace Institute's mission is: "To display all styles of artwork for students and the community to enjoy."

You may also choose from several cooperative galleries, run by artists, in which members share expenses and pay very small or no sales commissions (an advantage over most commercial galleries that charge 50% commission) in a less structured environment than commercial galleries. You will have a one-person exhibition approximately once every eighteen months plus group shows. Some cooperative galleries don't have a director in which case the artist members have to do their own gallery sitting, promotion and selling. Viridian Gallery, an excellent cooperative gallery, has Vernita Nemec as its director. Its mission is: "To offer artists the opportunity to do everything their way. It is not dictated by style, but rather by quality." NoHo Gallery, another highly recommended artist-run gallery does not have a director. It was established "To show diversity in esthetic concerns, styles and media." Many of its members are teachers in colleges and universities.

Art in General, a non-profit alternative space
"Role: To focus on the development of contemporary art
through its presentation – art that is often under-represented
in larger museum and commercial gallery structures."
From *The Complete Guide To New York Art Galleries*

Exhibitions for emerging artists are also possible through regional and national artist organizations that exhibit their members' work as well as offer non-member juried competitions. Among them are: The National Sculpture Society, The Pastel Society, The Salmagundi Club, The Brooklyn Watercolor Society, Burr Artists, Catharine Lorillard Wolfe Art Club, Westside Arts Coalition, American Society of Contemporary Artists, National Association of Women Artists, New York Society of Women Artists, and others. *(See Appendix II.)* Many public spaces welcome such artists' groups, such as Cork Gallery in Lincoln Center and National Arts Club. And, don't ignore New York's banks, libraries, bookstores, corporate spaces, restaurants and cafés that offer unique alternatives to galleries.

WHAT TO LOOK FOR IN A GALLERY

When seeking a gallery find one that shows work and prices that are compatible with yours. Look for a dealer who understands your work and expresses a commitment to it. Make sure you feel comfortable with him or her and are convinced the gallery will enhance your visibility and reputation. Before you make the leap keep abreast of the gallery's exhibitions and styles of art shown over several months, through reviews, advertisements, announcement cards and its web site. On your visits examine the lighting, gallery size and the way the art is presented. Observe how the personnel respond to visitors: They should be courteous and knowledgeable. Inquire about the gallery's reviewing process and level of interest in new artists. To find out how they promote their artists collect brochures and other documentation about them that is available at the front desk. Search the leading art magazines for advertisements placed by the gallery. Attend the opening receptions and notice the type of followers the gallery attracts and conducts business with. Observe how they treat the artists they represent.

June Kelly
"The gallery reviews new artists' materials in April.
Artists should mail slides or photos, résumé and SASE.
Art must show a unique vision, art with poetry and spirituality,
by artists who express their own vocabulary."
From *The Complete Guide To New York Art Galleries*

HOW TO APPROACH

An artist's desire to seek entry to the best galleries in New York – the art capital of the world – is easily understood. There is great value in having solid representation by a reputable New York dealer. Unfortunately, however, many artists make the mistake of approaching them prematurely. With illusions of achieving easy access to the highest tier of the gallery system they quickly learn it is a process that requires a methodical, persistent and serious approach, and it takes effort and time to develop – often beginning with the lower and middle rungs of the ladder. Dan Concholar, Director of the Art Information Center in New

York, has been advising artists on finding suitable galleries for their work for more than two decades. He says it takes at least seven years to penetrate the New York gallery system. If you are thinking of approaching top New York dealers, be persistent and learn how to cope with apathy and rejection. Build a strong body of work. Procure one-person exhibitions in respectable alternative spaces. Exhaust the best venues in your area – become "a big fish in a small pond." Build your assets, present your strengths and don't apologize for your weaknesses. The more you bring to the table – well-developed artwork, awards, fellowships, grants, positive reviews and loyal collectors of your art – the more leverage you have with the gallery. Many dealers' look at artists' work upon referrals so make an effort to establish relationships with the artists who are already in the gallery, and curators, critics, collectors or other dealers who are in the gallery's sphere of influence.

Gallery Henoch
"The best time for artists to submit materials is between January and February, and June and July. The artist must first familiarize themselves with the work the gallery represents."
From *The Complete Guide To New York Art Galleries*

You have probably realized that personal taste, personality and background, aesthetic concerns, collectors' demands, among others things, influence choice. Art dealer Mary Boone said, "Taste is a combination of a thousand different things that are known and unknown." Some dealers use phrases like "falling in love with the art" while others concentrate on the commercial value of the work. Most will agree that they seek professional behavior and commitment on behalf of the artists.

Most dealers are inundated by packages from a wide variety of artists on a weekly basis, many of which are inappropriate for the direction of the gallery. I encourage you to familiarize yourself with the shows they mount and the aesthetic direction they pursue before submitting materials for consideration. When they say they're "not looking" it may be because they schedule shows a year or two in advance and are focused on their current projects. My experience has taught me galleries "are looking" when the right work comes along. Smart dealers are always interested in artists who display outstanding talent and vision.

Nancy Hoffman Gallery
"We look at new artists' slides almost every Thursday.
Generally artists deliver slides in the AM
and pick up after 3:00".
From *The Complete Guide To New York Art Galleries*

The first step to finding an appropriate gallery is to conduct some research. Locate leads through *The Complete Guide To New York Art Galleries.* (You can use the order form in this book, go to www.ManhattanArts.com or call Manhattan Arts International 212-472-1660. It may also be obtained from the Museum of Modern Art or at Barnes and Noble and other stores.) Also read major magazines such as *Art in America, Artforum,* and *Gallery Guide.* Try to visit the galleries that interest you. If travel is difficult visit the galleries' web sites. Try to make contacts with other artists and art professionals in New York who can inform you about the galleries, the work they are showing and their reputation. Contrary to rumor, you don't have to move to New York in order to be exhibited by a New York gallery. However, unless you have someone you know very well serving as your representative in the same locale as the gallery, do not make a commitment with a gallery without seeing it and the owner face-to-face.

YOUR PRESENTATION

The gallery interviews up to 50 artist applicants in person and receives about 20 parcels of slides and photos in the mail each week, and visits the studios of those it considers to have works worthy of close inspection.
Ivan Karp, O.K. Harris Works of Art
From *The Complete Guide To New York Art Galleries*

The Complete Guide To New York Art Galleries lists the description of the galleries' viewing practices and required materials. A handful of galleries have open viewing days, such as Nancy Hoffman Gallery, whose policy is: "We look at new artists' slides almost every Thursday. Artists should leave slides in the gallery for review and pick them up later that day." George Adams' policy is: "Artists may bring their slides, photographs and résumé on Wednesday mornings at 9:15, October-April." Both galleries recommend calling the day before to confirm.

Most galleries prefer that the materials be sent in the mail. Your gallery presentation package should include your cover letter, résumé, slides or color prints and other visual documentation. They should be neatly organized in a pocket folder or binder. Indicate the size and subject of your work and medium. Your résumé should call attention to exhibitions, honors and awards, collections, reviews, art-related experience, and other achievements that enhance the value of your art. (For detailed advice and samples read the book *Presentation Power Tools For Fine Artists.* There is an order form in this book.

Most of the galleries request 10–20 color images. Instead of small slides I suggest you send larger color photographs, color Xerox or digital prints, especially if you are sending them for the first time without a referral. Your purpose is to introduce them to your work and stimulate interest. A color brochure or catalogue will make a great first impression. Color transparencies, CD-Roms and sometimes videos are also effective.

Although many galleries outside the New York area are more accommodating, cold walk-ins without an appointment are unappreciated in most New York galleries. However, I know an artist who was visiting from Texas who walked into a New York gallery, started a conversation with a sales person and asked if he could turn on his small notebook that contained a DVD of his artwork. His presentation made a very positive impression.

> *Art must be outstanding examples*
> *of the media, and aesthetically pleasing.*
> Multiple Impressions, Ltd.
> From *The Complete Guide To New York Art Galleries*

If you obtain an appointment with the gallery, do some homework before you go. Be prepared to discuss your work as well as the art in the gallery. Approach the experience as an opportunity to establish a relationship and your personal as well as professional attributes will be noticed. Find out as much as you can about the gallery and its owners in order to engage in a substantive dialogue. The book *The Complete Guide To New York Art Galleries* supplies helpful information about the gallery owner. For example, you would learn that gallery owner Annina Nosei has a doctorate in philosophy from the University of Rome and George Henoch Shechtman, owner of Gallery Henoch, was a painter who has a degree in art history from Rutgers University.

The most influential galleries are very selective (especially the members of the prestigious Art Dealers Association of America). By the time they become interested in an artist, he or she has probably had several one-person exhibitions. Paula Cooper said, "It takes me a long time to made the decision to start working with an artist, because it's a tremendous commitment, and I don't want to have to stop working with the artist, if possible."

Eighty percent of success is showing up.
Woody Allen

HANDLING REJECTION

If a gallery is only casually interested in looking at new artists' materials but your work fits their direction, instead of sending a bulk of materials, send one or more striking color sheets or a color brochure. Indicate that you would be pleased to send more materials if needed. Invite them to visit your studio. Keep them on your mailing list and abreast of your exhibitions. By keeping the lines of communication open, so when they are ready to add artists they will know about you.

When approaching galleries, don't think of it as a "pass" or "fail" situation. If the gallery doesn't accept your work on your first attempt, ask why, and for any ideas they may have about which galleries might be interested. Use the experience to gain some information. The prominent artist Jennifer Bartlett said: "I was disappointed that Paula Cooper didn't instantly offer me a one-woman show. But she gave three or four numbers to call." They may also want you to submit your materials again at a later date – to see how your work develops.

If you have difficulty getting a New York gallery you are in the company of hundreds of thousands of artists. The renowned artist Alex Katz wrote about his early years as an artist in *The New Art Examiner*: "One dealer... liked them well enough to put them in a closet. The dealer I liked best was Mrs. Kraushaar. She simply said these are too light for my gallery. I got to dislike people who said these are interesting, come back next year."

Don't be easily discouraged. With the confidence of knowing that you would be an asset to a gallery, make the selection with the utmost care, thoroughness and attention to detail. Pursue the galleries that are most appropriate, without placing too much emphasis on depending on any gallery for your success. If you focus on self-promotion and build a solid career history, the right galleries will be there for you when the time is right. If not, take comfort in the fact that many artists are enjoying successful careers without New York gallery representation. They have developed relationships with galleries in other parts of the world.

The next time you visit a gallery that shows work that is similar to yours, ask to see the artist's catalogue or artist's book. It is usually available to guests at the reception desk. Read it and compare your professional history with theirs. Look for leads to other exhibitions and collections of the artist. Approach the artists whose work you respect in the galleries you like and invite them to see your work. If you gained their interest and you become friends they may recommend you to their dealer.

THE IMPORTANCE OF BEING FOCUSED

One of the services I offer to artists is to examine and polish their presentation materials before I suggest appropriate galleries for them. Kim wanted to be represented by a New York gallery but wasn't having much success. She described a recent meeting with a dealer in which she presented a large portfolio representing her realistic watercolors, abstract assemblages and digital photographs. Kim lamented, "Although it seemed that her response was positive she didn't offer to take any of the work on consignment." Before our consultation I asked Kim to send me her promotional materials and a list of the galleries she had approached and their responses. I called the dealer who happened to be a personal friend of mine and asked her for her recollection of the meeting. She said Kim was talented but she lacked focus and said, "She hasn't yet found herself." The dealer was reluctant to establish a working relationship with her – to invest money and time in building her market and reputation – when she was uncertain which direction the artist was going.

Kim learned an invaluable lesson. She continues to experiment with new media and shows her work in alternative spaces. When she approaches a commercial gallery she arranges her portfolio in a more focused manner. She considers the gallery's aesthetic direction and brings a compatible, solid body of work.

Success comes from concentrating on being an expert in one area. Think about it: If Betsy Johnson designed funky clothes one day and tailored clothes the next would she be as successful? Would Elvis have become the idol he is if he alternated between opera and rock? If Deepak Chopra failed to provide a consistent message throughout his books would he be a best selling spiritual author? Leaders in their fields know how to specialize or "brand" themselves. They etch their styles in the minds of consumers. A style can be explained as a consistent feeling that your potential customer feels from you and your work. It is not only seen it is experienced. Take for example the work of Thomas Kinkade, the "Painter of Light." When we view his work, we are not only viewing a scene, we are feeling tranquility and inspiration.

USE PROTECTION

A verbal contract isn't worth the paper it's written on.
Louis B. Mayer

Having your work in a New York gallery does not guarantee instant success. It also does not guarantee that your work will sell, or the gallery won't move to a different location, go bankrupt, decide to change its marketing direction, or take a partner who will come with his or her own artists. Statistics prove that only a small number of artists have the kind of dealers and arrangements that can sustain their reputations and finances for many years. I encourage you to think that only the best will happen but I also encourage you to use protection.

John was a major artist whom I met at a gallery opening and I was surprised when he asked me if I could recommend a gallery for him. I assumed he was still represented by one of the leading uptown blue-chip galleries. I then learned that the gallery wasn't taking his new work, although his earlier work was selling in the high five-figure range in the secondary market. (Since New York does not have resale laws to protect artists, John was not receiving a penny from resales.)

A few months later this talented, trusting, gentle man went to his grave financially poor. Why? My guess is he relied on the gallery to take care of business for him indefinitely and he failed to provide future plans. He didn't take care of business. I regret that I didn't meet him earlier to help him avoid this situation.

Select your gallery wisely and keep a close contact with your dealers. Don't put all of your faith in one gallery. Be careful that you do not become so blinded by your present situation – no matter how good it is – that you fail to make plans for the future.

Before you begin a relationship with a dealer discuss a range of issues – from the duration of the representation to their payment procedure – and get a written contract. It is always best to iron out any disagreements in the beginning rather than having to dispute them later with feelings of resentment and confusion. In many business relationships, it is not necessarily intentional dishonesty that causes problems as much as the misinterpretation of a verbal agreement or the absence of communication.

A sample Artist/Gallery Agreement, a sample Consignment Agreement and a long list of important questions to ask a dealer are offered in my book *Presentation Power Tools For Fine Artists. (See order form on page 237.)* I also recommend *Business and Legal Forms for Fine Artists* by Tad Crawford. Since many galleries use a contract that their lawyers have drafted to protect their interests, it is essential for you to obtain legal counseling before signing a contract.

Check the gallery's references through the Better Business Bureau and Attorney General's office. Contact artist organizations in their area and ask if they have received any complaints. If the gallery is located in New York you may contact me to inquire about its reputation.

Artist shall contribute $6,500 upon the signing of
this agreement at his/her share of financial responsibility...
From A New York Gallery Contract

SHOULD YOU PAY TO PLAY?

On a regular basis I receive calls, letters and e-mails from artists asking me about New York galleries that charge artists fees to exhibit their work. These fees can be as high as several thousand dollars. I have seen a number of fee-paid galleries (also known as "vanity" galleries) come and go over the last two decades. Galleries that charge fees for exhibitions seem to have multiplied in recent years. I maintain a growing file containing copies of their pitch letters and contracts. I am sure that I will be responding to these questions as long as there are artists in need of exposure within the galleries that operate in this manner.

While legitimate galleries focus on producing buyers and obtaining recognition for their artist these galleries prey on the vulnerability of artists who desire a gallery exhibition, at practically any cost. They are very aggressive in their sales pitches to artists. Many of them have become very adept at luring the naïve artist with the right buzzwords and sales psychology. Their advertisements appear where artists are likely to look for exhibition opportunities. Some of them advertise competitions for which the "winners" are eligible to exhibit in the gallery at a fee. They act interested in the artist's work but their interest wanes if the artist doesn't want to "pay to play."

Many artists who have taken this route have complained to me that the fees they paid far outweighed the benefits. They observed that these galleries in general lack marketing and promotion skills. They often behave in a condescending manner toward the artist, acting as though they were doing them a favor, instead of giving him or her the respect they deserve. They often refuse to share information about the buyer if any work is sold. In the worst instances the galleries pack up and leave town without notifying the artists or returning their work. I have been called upon more than once to intervene on behalf of the artist in order to retrieve money or art. Unfortunately, most artists are too embarrassed to report their problems to the Better Business Bureau or Attorney General's Office and that makes it difficult for other artists to build a case against the galleries.

Showcase fee... price for Gallery I... 80 feet... $8,400...
from a New York gallery contract

When vanity galleries open for business the word spreads quickly within the art community. When we learn that a gallery charges artists to pay for exhibitions we add the information to their listing in *The Complete Guide To New York Art Galleries* in order to give artists advance warning. A critic friend of mine said whenever he notices a vanity gallery on an artist's résumé it tells him the artist is paying to get their ego stroked.

Whether or not you pay for a show is your choice, but I advise you to make the decision with your head, not your emotions. Carefully examine the pitfalls and expenses. What are your risks for this investment? How much do you have to sell in order to cover your expenses? Don't forget to add up all of your costs including shipping, insurance, framing and traveling.

If you should acquiesce to a fee-paid gallery, before paying a penny, *get everything that was promised to you in writing.* Make sure the contract includes your entitlements such as a partial or full refund if the gallery fails to live up to their end of the agreement. You are entitled to services rendered, have your questions answered and receive professional respect. If you don't get it, place your checkbook back in your pocket and run! Then, please contact me with the information so I can include it in my files. You will not only be doing yourself a favor, but helping other artists as well.

If your work has merit and you are an ambitious self-promoter you have many alternatives to paying to show. Invest your money in printing a brochure, procuring a mailing list to cultivate direct sales, hiring an administrative assistant, or consulting a publicist to build your media exposure. Join a cooperative gallery, hold "Open Studio" events, and explore the myriad of alternative exhibition spaces in the United States and abroad.

DOES IT EVER PAY TO PAY?

If you have been trying to get an exhibition without success you may argue that paying for one offers a quick solution. You may say a New York show will give your career a jump-start. If you are an artist from a foreign country you may claim that having an exhibition in New York will give you instant success at home.

Kirsten was an artist from Germany whose paintings were selling in galleries there for $10,000. Her German collectors were urging her to have a New York gallery exhibition, so she asked me to locate one that would give her a show within six months. It is very rare, if not impossible, for any gallery to have an opening within a short period of time, but I knew of one that could accommodate her. It was a large gallery in a prominent street-level location in SoHo, but it required a substantial deposit against sales. After we discussed the advantages and disadvantages she decided to proceed.

Her contacts in New York were limited, so she enlisted my services for a mailing list, publicity and promotion. The director of the gallery did no more than serve as a gracious hostess at the opening reception. A few of Kirsten's collectors flew in from Germany and made purchases, which covered the gallery fee and my counseling services. As a result of one of my contacts, Kirsten was invited to exhibit in a group show at a museum. An art dealer in a major uptown gallery later invited her to participate in a group show.

For Kirsten the exhibition was a success, however, the results may not have been the same if she didn't have the loyalty of several well-endowed German buyers, a well-planned, ambitious promotional campaign, and a substantial financial budget to finance the exhibition.

Questions to Ask
Before Taking the Plunge

If there is a gallery that has expressed interest in showing your work and requires a financial investment and you are tempted to take the plunge, please follow this advice. Visit it routinely over a period of at least two seasons, at different times of the day. Attend their receptions. Compare their style of doing business with established galleries that are known for building their artists' reputations. Check the Better Business Bureau, Attorney General's office and artists' organizations for any complaints. Contact me if the gallery is in New York. Then, the following questions should be answered to your satisfaction before exhibiting in *any* gallery – fees or no fees.

- Is the gallery genuinely impressed with your work (or your ability to pay the fee) and have they told you why?
- Does the gallery offer a contract that obligates them to perform specific services *for you* or does the contract serve only to protect *them?*
- What do you hope to achieve from this venture? What role will this exhibition play in your overall career objectives?
- What do the leading critics, gallery owners, artists' organizations and fellow artists say about the gallery? Has the gallery received any legitimate reviews by known critics?
- If you pay a dealer a substantial sum upfront, do you think they will be motivated to develop sales of your work?
- Does the gallery consistently advertise in art publications for "Call For Artists" and "Competitions"? Think about this: If they were satisfying their artists through sales and promotion why do they need to pitch to more artists?
- Do they offer tangible public relations and marketing services? When you ask for specific proofs of past performance, do they respond with concrete evidence?
- Do they treat you in a condescending manner as though you should be grateful to them for giving you the opportunity?
- Is the gallery in a favorable location? What is the appearance and attitude of the gallery and staff? Is the hanging and lighting properly arranged?
- Is the quality of the artwork unprofessional or uneven in quality?
- Are too many pieces hung on the wall too close together without sufficient space in between them?
- Have you observed any qualified buyers in the gallery? Are there mostly artists at their receptions or does the gallery have a respected following of art consultants, interior designers, architects, collectors and members of the press?

- Who determines the price of your work? When will you be notified of sales? How soon do you get paid after the sale? Will the dealer release names and addresses of those who buy your work?
- If the gallery is offering you extended representation, how many exhibitions are they offering in one year? What are the costs and obligations for each?
- What month(s) are they offering you? (In New York, January, February, July and August are the least desirable times.)
- What kind of effort do they make to sell the work? A good gallery knows not to rely on walk-in traffic for sales; they generate sales through persistent effort – phone calls, press releases, advertising, mailings and a range of networking activities.
- What portion of your fee goes toward advertising? What types of advertising (radio, TV, or print) do they buy on a regular basis?
- Do they invite you to have a role in the decision-making process about where and how they spend *your* money? Are they overstating their costs?
- Who will pay for invitations, receptions and advertising?
- How many of their artists have remained with them for more than five years? Do you know any artists in the gallery whose work has sold in it? What complaints do their artists have?

The artist shall contribute the following fees towards advertising,
catalogue, public relations... $28,000
from a New York gallery contract

RECORD OF GALLERY LEADS & STATUS REPORT

When you contact a gallery keep a record of the materials you sent and to whom, the date sent and the response.

_____

_____

_____

_____

_____

_____

_____

_____

_____

_____

_____

_____

_____

_____

_____

_____

_____

_____

_____

_____

_____

_____

_____

_____

CHAPTER 8

FINDING YOUR BUYERS & BUILDING YOUR MARKETS

Today it is the artists who pull the strings, not the dealers...
the artists are selling themselves at this point.
Ileana Sonnabend

Marketing is a term we associate with Madison Avenue advertising executives, however, it is not a new concept. In the book *Archaic and Classical Greek Art* by Robin Osborne, published by Oxford University Press, there is a chapter titled "Marketing an Image." It refers to the export market in the beginning of the sixth century, when the Greek mainland potters created pottery to compete with markets nearby and far away.

Then, as now, when an individual decides to sell an item the marketing process begins. When you advertise your exhibition, and consider the publication's readership, demographics and circulation, that is an aspect of marketing. When you look for a gallery, agent or web site to sell your work you that is market research. When you choose a mat, frame or pedestal for your work, you are considering a crucial part of market presentation.

People do not buy art because they think they *need* it, they buy it because they *want* it. Have you given any thought to *who* will *want* to buy your work? Many artists are mystified about determining *who* to target their sales and *how, when* and *where* to reach them. This chapter shows you the steps to take that will lead you in the right direction. Apply just a few ideas and techniques offered in this chapter and you will be on the way to increasing your following and increasing your bank account.

To begin learning about how art is marketed visit successful galleries, art fairs, artists' open studios and art auctions. Observe how art is displayed, sold and talked about. Examine sizes and comparative prices. Read art magazines and study the advertisements and reviews. Which artists are more popular and why? Take workshops and read books on the subject of marketing.

Art among a religious group produces reliques;
among a military one, trophies;
among a commercial one, articles of trade.
Henry Fuseli

THE DISTINCTIVE QUALITIES OF YOUR WORK

To determine *who* your potential buyers are it is helpful to fully understand the distinctive qualities of your work. How does it stand out from art being created today? How and why does your work appeal to others? How do your buyers describe your work? Why is your work desirable? What adjectives do you use to describe it? Is it miniature, intimate, large, universal, abstract, realistic, digital, geometric, impressionistic, mixed-media, surrealistic, conservative, traditional, cutting edge, primitive, decorative, endearing, shocking, tactile, visceral, intellectual, psychological, political, historical, visionary or healing? Is it related to technology, nature, animal, biology, astronomy, people, culture, science or history? Does it involve the use of unique materials, concepts, technology or vision? With this information you can begin to find your best customers and market position or *niche*.

Write the distinctive attributes of your work below:

_____

_____

_____

_____

_____

_____

_____

_____

WHO ARE YOUR BUYERS?
WHAT IS YOUR CUSTOMER PROFILE?

To determine your customer profile, ask these questions: Who are the individuals, businesses, organizations and periodicals that relate best to your work? Where and how do they live? Are they city or rural dwellers? Do they fit into a primary educational, ethnic, gender, age group, religious or professional group? Where do they buy their art? What periodicals do they read? Where do they spend their vacations? What are their hobbies? When you develop your customer profile you will discover many paths to sales, commissioned work, projects and exhibition and publicity opportunities. You will be able to focus on the most appropriate market venues.

ARTISTS WHO KNOW HOW
TO REACH THE BUYERS

- Maria is a California artist whose paintings pay homage to the laborers of Latin America. She selected the most popular four images to create prints and devised a color flier welcoming inquiries from dealers and buyers. She procured a target market list from the biographical directory *Who's Who in the Latin American Community* to whom she mailed the fliers with order forms. This marketing plan led to several university and museum exhibitions and hundreds of sales.

- David's work has a nautical theme so he approached galleries that specialize in nautical artwork. He also exhibits and sells his work in marinas, seafood businesses and restaurants. To build his market he looks for leads in yachting magazines and pursues those businesses that appear in them.

- Eva specializes in children's portraits. She taps into the manufacturers and retail stores of children's toys and clothing in addition to publishers, private and public schools, day care centers and orphanages. Her marketing attempts range from giving art demonstrations in toy stores to donating a portrait at a fund-raiser for an orphanage. She sometimes places a cooperative ad with a children's clothing store.

- Akiko's subject matter reflects social and political issues. The market niche uses to get her message to buyers consists of political and social action groups, universities, alternative learning centers, special interest groups, grant givers and publications that cover the same issues. As she develops relationships with them many of the groups are willing to share their connections and mailing lists with her.

- Bracha is a pet portrait artist whose potential buyers and avenues of promotion include pet owners, breeders, pet groomers, pet food manufacturers, animal shows, pet magazines, greeting card and calendar publishers, and the Franklin Mint – to name a few.

- Milenka creates large, colorful, abstract paintings. Her market venues are hotel lobbies, restaurants and other public spaces in addition to private homes. Her market leads include architects, corporate art consultants and interior designers.
- Kendal's subjects are still life and florals. His market leads include botanical associations, horticulturists, flower clubs, flower shops, flower seed distributors and catalogues in addition to the local and national chapters of interior design organizations.

LIST YOUR LEADS TO MARKETS & BUYERS

_____

_____

_____

_____

_____

_____

_____

_____

_____

_____

_____

_____

_____

_____

My favorite clients have always been the ones who collect out of
love, just as children collect postage stamps; you fall in love with
things that delight you, that you can't resist.
Betty Parsons

WHY DO COLLECTORS BUY ART?

Ask a collector and they might say that the act of collecting it is not about accumulating, nor is it about investing. The serious collector might say it is based upon following their instinct, taste, passion, preference and study that leads to acquiring objects that build a collection of works that are somehow related to each other. In the dictionary you'll find the definition of the word collect as: "To bring together in a group; gather; assemble." When the collection is assembled (which is an on-going process for the collector) it brings a value beyond the sum of the parts, it creates a certain order and reflection of the collector's response to them. Quite often when a collector buys a piece they might be secretly asking themselves how the new piece will fit in with the others they own or if it will fill a historical or stylistic gap in their collection.

A resource to help you understand what motivates collectors is *ARTnews'* annual issue devoted to "Top Collectors" and their collections. You should know who these collectors are and the nature of their collections. You may discover among them a few collectors that will buy emerging artists' work. But, don't limit the collectors to this select few. When your work is for sale for a few hundred or few thousand dollars, the field is wide open. For your purposes, you should define "collectors" as any individuals or companies that may be interested in your work and are willing to pay the price you ask.

Success is what sells. Andy Warhol

How to Meet Collectors

Buyers of your work are all around you. They are your neighbors, relatives and friends. They are the blue collar workers and the people you read about in the social columns. They are people and businesses that will come to you and those you must reach. Strive to develop a coterie of supporters to help you spread the word that your work is available. Make it easy for art buyers to find you.

You don't have to win over a huge percentage of the population to be hugely successful. If you made your art known to just one-tenth of 1% of the population in the U.S., you'd have more than 280,000 prospective buyers. How do you meet them?

- Join the best local art museum at the highest membership category you can afford. You'll benefit from the opportunity to socialize at the museum's private receptions and use of private dining room and other membership amenities.
- Sign the guest book mailing list of the best galleries and attend their openings.
- Join cultural institutions, community service organizations, or the Junior League.
- Interview collectors for your community or arts publication.
- Open your studio to clubs, charities and tour groups.
- Make appearances and give talks about your work in colleges, business organizations and hospitals.
- Get a job in a gallery or work for a successful artist.
- Form or join an arts organization and invite collectors, curators and critics to jury your exhibitions.
- Look for leads in business reference and national and international biographical reference books, such as *Who's Who* Directories, which can be found at the public library.

Your Marketing Tools

- **Business Card:** This is the most basic and least expensive tool but for an artist it is useless unless you feature an image of your work on it.
- **Postcard:** This tool features a larger image of your work and is easy to mail or hand out for any occasion.
- **Sales Sheet:** An effective sales tool is an 8-1/2" x 11" color sheet with one or more images displayed on it with your contact information and a brief biography and artist's statement.
- **Brochure:** This impressive tool contains several pages and takes your art to a higher level.

Visit galleries and expositions for samples and ideas. The office supply store sells perforated cards and scored brochure paper if you want to print these tools from your desktop. When selecting a commercial printer shop around for competitive prices. The book *Presentation Power Tools for Fine Artists* offers step-by-step advice on preparing marketing tools and contains many samples. *(There is an order form in this book.)*

How to Create Your Mailing List

Your mailing list is an essential component of your marketing program. Keep it clean, make it grow and use it often. Since people move and forwarding orders expire, do at least three mailings a year. Computer programs such as ACT!, and Microsoft Access (which our business uses) provide efficient ways to maintain your list and progress. Get some help if you detest computer work.

Your mailing list begins with relatives, friends, professional associates and everyone who has ever bought your work or expressed an interest in it. Add to your list your attorney, dentist, doctor and accountant, other artists, instructors, framers and art supply stores. Include those individuals who should know about your work such as art gallery owners and other retailers, board members of non-profit organizations, slide registries, museum directors, residencies, foundations, curators, corporate art consultants, newspaper and magazine writers and critics.

Any fool can paint a picture,
but it takes a wise man to be able to sell it.
Samuel Butler

How to Increase Your Mailing List

- Use guest books at your exhibitions and "Open Studios."
- Have a box or bowl in the exhibition space and invite guests to enter their business card for a chance to win a prize.
- When you advertise your artwork in a magazine or newspaper offer readers something free upon request such as a brochure or future exhibition schedule.
- Look for leads of prospective buyers in the social columns of the newspapers and upscale magazines.
- Read *Crain's New York Business'* annual "Top Business Lists" that has names and addresses of the 100 highest paid executives; leading architectural, accounting and law firms; advertising agencies; banks; and fastest-growing firms.
- Circulate your promotional materials in banks, schools, libraries, concierge desks in luxury hotels, mailrooms of luxury apartment buildings, gourmet shops, pedigree dog groomers, tanning salons, spas, beauty salons and travel agencies.

- Search the Internet, telephone directories, biographical directories and general and special interest periodicals.
- Find upscale organizations that sell their membership directories such as the American Society of Interior Designers.
- Purchase mailing lists from Artist Help Network at www.artisthelpnetwork.com operated by Caroll Michels, author of *How To Survive and Prosper As An Artist.*

Soft cover presentation books
with plastic sleeves are valuable tools.
Advice from Frances P. Harris, Art Advisor

THE CORPORATE CHALLENGE

A corporation's interest in art is most often to build a collection of work that adheres to the highest standards, while it also must consider the needs and style of its own corporate personality. Your work may be very suitable for corporate collections if it addresses two or more of the following needs: Does it reflect and enhance the corporate image of the company? Does it decorate the walls and improve the working environment and productivity? Does it fulfill the percent-for-law requirements? Does it qualify as a sound investment? Is it pleasing to the eye? Does it boost morale?

In addition to providing these assets to the corporation, the purchase of the art must appease the stockholders, who often look askance at buying art as an unnecessary expense, and the art must satisfy the employees who might prefer that the money be spent on salary hikes. Especially now, with corporate downsizing so prevalent, corporations that are cutting out jobs do not want to appear as if they're spending too much money on art.

Corporations use one of two methods for developing their collections. They either have inside personnel that buy art directly from artists and galleries, or they hire outside corporate art consultant firms that specialize in providing art for companies.

Don't be timid about contacting corporations directly. Obtain information from the switchboard of the company's policy about collecting art. Find out the name of the art director, art consultant, public relations manager or corporate communications director. Inquire into the nature of the program and the appropriate way to make one's work known. When you speak to the individual in charge, find out what materials are required and what kind of art they're looking for.

You can learn about America's most active corporate collections in *Art & Auction* and *Art & Antiques* magazines and you can purchase corporate art consultant mailing lists, but don't limit yourself to targeting established collections. Look for new companies that are moving into your neighborhood. Contact companies that already own your work to find out if they are expanding in size or building new offices. Contact architects and interior designers who have new corporate clients.

When approaching corporations and corporate art consultants, you should be prepared with the benefits your art will have on the work environment and how it will enhance the company's mission. The same way you would link the special qualities of your work with the similar tastes of individuals and with gallery owners, you will determine the types of businesses that would respond favorably to your work. Interviews with business owners will inform you of their tastes and the kind of image they want to project. Articles and advertisements are excellent leads to prospective business buyers. Prospects can be found in general and special interest publications.

In addition to slides and photographs of your work you should consider sending photo CDs to corporate art consultants. They are gaining in popularity, as more people are using computers with photo CDs for both professional and home use. The disks may also be sent to individual art collectors as well as dealers and require less postage than a package of slides and other materials.

Don't be easily discouraged. At first, you might have to start small. Marge is a successful artist who began selling her limited edition prints to companies. Gradually, the corporate executives and employees expressed an interest in seeing her originals. She is now selling her paintings to them and no longer depends on the prints for financial support.

To break the ice, many artists begin their corporate sales through friends and relatives who place their artwork in their places of business through sales or gifts. When your work enters a collection include your corporate collectors on your résumé.

ADVICE FROM
FRANCES P. HARRIS: ART ADVISOR

Frances P. Harris is a Principal of Blumberg & Harris, Inc. Established in 1980, Blumberg & Harris, Inc. is an art / management advisory firm located in New York City and Philadelphia, working with corporate and private collections, galleries, museums and artists. The firm specializes in advising corporations and private collectors in developing art collections. They are independent advisors serving the interests of their clients by selecting the best art without bias because there is no conflict of interest. They have no inventory and they do not represent any specific artists. They select works of the highest quality in a vari-

ety of media including paintings, sculptures, photographs and prints for purchase, installation, framing and cataloguing. They also select the art for making verbal presentations and organizing exhibitions. Their many clients include MBNA Corporation, Newark, DE; Home Life Insurance Company, New York, NY; CIGNA Corporation, Philadelphia, PA; McCarter and English, Newark, NJ, to name a few.

She advises artists to make lists of corporate advisors, curators, consultants, designers and architects and submit the following:

- Slides, photo CDs, videos and other visuals (these can be used for presentations on a larger scale).
- Soft cover presentation books with plastic sleeves (11 ½ " x 9 ½") to show laser prints or photographs of recent artwork and all details – title, medium and dimensions. These books are valuable tools for small meetings and to show private collectors. Include updated résumé, press articles and an artist's statement.
- In addition to the printed materials your web site also offers an excellent tool.
- If possible, include any letters of recommendation you have received or an introduction from an art professional.
- Self-addressed stamped envelope.
- If you think the targeted prospect is of importance to you send package by Priority Mail or Express Delivery to receive attention.

She adds the following "Do Not" tips:

- Do not be discouraged if visuals are returned. This is not a reflection on the work, but a specific project or client for which the work might not be suitable. Remember, you are dealing with consultants / advisors – not galleries.

- Do not call or e-mail to invite them to your studio. If they are interested in a studio visit you'll certainly be contacted.
- Do not mention that the slides or visuals you have do not do your work justice. Make sure you have the appropriate material to present your work to its best advantage.

The best way to have a good idea is to have a lot of ideas.
Linus Pauling

EXPAND AND DIVERSIFY YOUR MARKETS

In addition to selling to different groups of buyers expand your markets by offering different price levels. For instance, in addition to selling higher priced original art, introduce lower priced limited edition prints and drawings. Sell smaller canvases as well as larger canvases. Sell photographs and videos of your installations. Sell small sculpture or wearable art jewelry in addition to your larger bronzes. Give buyers a taste of your talent and they will most likely return for larger and more expensive pieces.

With the help of new technology you can expand your market with high-resolution digital also called Iris Prints or Giclées that can be reproduced on acid-free watercolor paper, stretched canvas or other surfaces. Coatings may be applied to increase water resistance. Artists are creating "embellished prints" by adding paint or other media on the surface of the prints. One of the advantages of digital prints is that you can order small quantities. The longevity, techniques and costs vary from printer to printer so query them and look for referrals from satisfied customers. To learn more on the subject see periodicals such as *Art Business News* and attend trade shows such as International Art Expo New York.

Explore the licensing market, especially if your work has mass appeal. Have you been told, "Your animal sculptures would make interesting collectibles"? Maybe fans of your colorful paintings have said, "I'd love to see them in bed linens." Perhaps you have considered producing calendars and note cards. It seems like every shop window contains a plethora of products – from the newest version of the pet rock to high-end collectibles. You can't help but think there is an artist behind the product who is dancing all the way to the bank. Charles Riotto, president of the International Licensing Industry Merchandisers' Association says, "Artists realize that licensing their original artwork enables them to generate royalties far beyond a one-time purchase fee."

Andrew Abrams, also known as Agent Andy, is a licensing agent for creative individuals with new product ideas and designs. His web site is www.IamCreative.com. He advises, "Your business planning should start with market information. Without knowledge of competitive products and prices, industry players, and current trends, you are running blind. One of the best places to gather strategic information is at regional trade shows. There are many around the country that showcase giftware, decorative accessories, stationery products, and fabrics that are based on two- and three-dimensional artwork. Trade shows are loaded with experienced sales and marketing advisors. Pick their brains and observe how and what they are selling. Trade magazines, are excellent sources of information, and their editors are usually the most market-savvy individuals."

The L!CENSING International show takes place at Jacob K. Javits Convention Center, in June. For more information go to, www.licensingshow.com. *Li©ense!* is a trade magazine with an informative web site at www.Licensemagazine.com.

87 MARKET LEADS FROM A TO Z

1. Accountants
2. Airports
3. Animal rights groups
4. Architects
5. Art consultants
6. Art organizations
7. Art publishers
8. Banks
9. Book publishers
10. Botanical clubs
11. Boutiques
12. Bus terminals
13. Chambers of Commerce
14. Charities
15. Churches
16. Commissioned works
17. Consulates
18. Corporations
19. Country clubs
20. Cruise ships
21. Community centers
22. Dance halls
23. Day care centers
24. Dog breeders
25. Diners
26. Doctor's offices
27. Educational organizations
28. Embassies
29. Entertainment clubs
30. Fairs/Festivals
31. Franklin Mint
32. Federal Halls
33. Fire stations
34. Fitness clubs
35. Flower shops
36. Framers
37. Furniture showrooms
38. Galleries
39. Gift shops
40. Gov't agencies
41. Greeting card publishers
42. Guilds
43. Hair Salons
44. Hotels
45. Hospitals
46. Holistic centers
47. Health spas
48. Insurance agents
49. Interior designers
50. Internet
51. Juried competitions
52. Law offices
53. Libraries
54. Mail order catalogues
55. Marinas
56. Medical facilities
57. Model homes
58. Motels
59. Museums
60. Night clubs
61. Nursing homes
62. "Open Studios"
63. Orphanages
64. Periodicals
65. Pet shops
66. Print publishers
67. Real estate brokers
68. Resorts
69. Restaurants
70. Senior centers
71. Slide registries
72. Spas
73. Specialty markets
74. Store windows
75. Subway stations
76. Swim clubs
77. Synagogues
78. Tanning salons
79. Teacher's lounges
80. Trade shows
81. Travel agencies
82. Universities
83. Web sites
84. *Who's Who* directories
85. Wineries
86. Yard sales
87. Zoos

CHAPTER 9

HOW TO SELL YOUR ART

There's no such thing as "hard sell" and "soft sell."
There is only "smart sell" and "stupid sell."
Leo Burnett

The thought of selling may make your stomach turn and cause your heart to palpitate. You may envision loud, street corner hawkers, obnoxious, fast-talking car salesmen or politicians or pushy women behind the cosmetic counter – all making false promises. This is the last type of person you want to become. You would prefer spending your time negotiating the aesthetics of color, design, form and texture rather than discussing the benefits of your work to a prospective buyer.

During those blissful years in art school, probably none of your teachers prepared you for the dilemma of selling your work. If it is an unpleasant experience for you, try to approach the process by thinking that when you sell your work you are offering someone the opportunity to own something that will enrich his or her life. Selling is an enjoyable process of sharing and exchanging your art for money and recognition. The sale of your work perpetuates the circle of communication – perhaps one of the incentives for you to be an artist. Money earned from work that has been sold might offer you financial freedom from a mundane job or an unhappy marriage. As your sales grow, so will your confidence and reassurance. I'm sure you can think of many more rewards gained from the pleasure of selling.

For artists, there has never been a better time for them to sell their work directly to art buyers. The factors that influence the art market have changed dramatically over the decades. During the '60's and '70's, many people bought art to hedge against inflation. "The '80's Boom" was characterized by high prices and over-valued art caused by over-zealous dealers. It led to what may be called "The '90's Bust", when prices dipped with the economy and many art buyers ran away from dealers. In the current decade we are seeing more educated buyers who are confident about buying directly from artists. There is more direct interaction between artists and art buyers with the growth of web sites and "Open Studios." Artists are also more assertive.

INCREASE SALES
BY REJECTING SOME MYTHS

MYTH: "IN ORDER TO SELL I HAVE TO BE AGGRESSIVE."

Not true. Hard-selling, aggressive tactics are distasteful and ineffective. The best salespeople don't use coercion to close a sale, rather they place their customer's interests and desires ahead of their own. The best sales traits are confidence, sincerity, knowledge, politeness, enthusiasm, and empathy. The best artists aim to make the selling experience comfortable for the buyer.

They express passion for their art and employ modest self-promotion methods.

Everyone lives by selling something.
Robert Lewis Stevenson

MYTH: "I WASN'T BORN AS A SALESPERSON."

The truth is, all of us engage in some form of selling every-day. For example, when we try to persuade a friend to get a flu shot, see a particular movie or eat in our favorite restaurant, we are using a form of selling. As we well know, some of us are more skilled in the art of persuasion than others. To become better at selling your art it helps to understand why people make decisions about their purchases. In "Top Secrets", an article by Brian Tracy in *Entrepreneur* magazine by Brian Tracy says, "People don't buy products or services; they buy the results (or benefits) they expect to experience by using your product or service." Artwork certainly elicits a range of experiences.

To improve your selling skills show interest and ask your prospective buyer questions, listen to their responses to learn more about them – their lifestyles, where they come from, likes and dislikes, art they already own, how they decorate their homes, favorite artists and hobbies. Engage them in conversation by asking: "What style or color are you looking for?" "What room are you thinking about bringing art to?" "What is the room used for?" Is this a gift or for your home?" "Does this painting appeal to you more than that one?" "Would this sculpture fit your room?" Would you like to pay by check or credit card?"

Become skillful by observing the behavior of excellent sales teachers and adopt those skills that make you feel most comfortable. The best techniques are those that feel natural to you. Ask your friends if you can practice with them.

MYTH: "THE ART SHOULD SELL BY ITSELF."

This is one of the biggest myths. Visit any successful gallery and observe the way art is sold. The best dealers are not standing idly waiting for visitors. They are busy selling on the phone, attending business meetings or having lunch with prospective buyers or curators. For art to be sold it is praised for its tangible and intangible merits. Not everyone understands art or has confidence in their own judgment, which is why they seek the counsel of art advisors, dealers and other collectors. As an artist, you can encourage them to trust their responses to your work. Create and distribute the best quality promotional materials that you can afford – brochures, fliers, color postcards and/or folded cards. The book *Presentation Power Tools For Fine Artists* offers many ideas and samples. *(There is an order form in this book.)*

Buyers may not relate to your work in the same manner in which it was created. Their reasons for buying art run the gamut from matching the carpet to acquiring social status. Understanding the laws of psychology can be helpful if you want to increase your sales. Theoretically people are primarily either left-brained (logical) or right-brained (creative). Left-brained people are receptive to logical information and respond to the kind of sales techniques that gives them ten reasons to buy. (Such as: "One of the ten reasons why you should buy this painting is... her work is in the Chase Collection.") Right-brained people are more receptive to emotional and aesthetic appeals ("Look at how the sky and pasture in this painting evoke a sense of peace and harmony…"). *(Also see the chapter Rejection is a Matter of Perspective.)*

There are no dumb customers. Peter Drucker

MYTH: "ONLY RICH PEOPLE BUY ART."

Don't believe it! As an artist I must have sold hundreds of pieces of my work directly to individuals. More than twenty years later, I can vividly recall two of my most memorable sales. One was to an eighty year-old woman, living on a fixed-income, and the other was to a sixteen year-old student who came from a low-income family. My paintings were their first art purchases.

I will never forget the look of bliss on the face of the elderly woman when she stood in front of my landscape painting. With tears in her eyes she told me how much the painting reminded her of a place she knew as a child. The memory brought her tremendous solace and she bought it without hesitation. I will always cherish the special bond we shared.

The young student who bought one of my seascape paintings took a part-time job to pay for it. She came to my studio every week with her payments so she could visit her painting. When she paid in full, she invited me to her home to see the special place where she hung the work. To my surprise, it was the only original work of art in the entire house.

If I had prejudged these individuals these sales and many others would not have occurred. I would have also missed the joy these people brought to my life. They made an indelible impression on me.

If art is to survive as an important language,
it will be through the persistent will of artists
and through models chosen from among themselves.
Harold Rosenberg

SUCCESSFUL SELLING STRATEGIES

- Susan knows that industry-related businesses make excellent clients. She sold several of her paintings of European scenes to a travel agency for their corporate offices. Their satellite offices sell her framed, limited edition prints right from the walls and give them as gifts to their best customers. Keeping in mind the importance of targeting her market, she advertises her art in travel and hotel magazines.

- In time for holiday gift-giving every November a cooperative gallery presents a "Small Works Holiday Show" with every work of art priced below $250. Each year they select a children's charity to which they contribute a portion of the proceeds. Many of the sales transpire because of the goodwill behind the event. The buyer gains a beautiful work of art and a portion of the sale price is tax deductible.

- Bill inserts his announcement cards for his exhibitions in envelopes when he pays his bills and makes donations. This method has brought him sales and other kinds of opportunities, such as an offer to present a slide lecture.

- Doug created a series of mixed media abstract works that were inspired by computerized images. To create excitement and interest in his work he assigned titles to them that industry professionals would relate to, such as "Bytes", "External Bay", and "Interface." He approached every computer-related company in his area and landed several exhibitions and sales. He also selected one of his most popular designs and had it printed on mouse pads with his name, e-mail and web site. He sells them and gives them as gifts to his customers.

- To increase attendance at his exhibitions and prospective buyers when Eduardo sends his announcement cards he features a reproduction of one of his black and white drawings and invites his guests to color it and bring it to the opening reception. His guests are always curious to see his drawing hanging in the show and to compare it with theirs.

- Robert paints large, abstract paintings. When his friends were trying to sell their house he hung his art throughout their house to be viewed by the real estate brokers as well as prospective buyers and offered his friends a commission. He left his business cards and brochures available to those who attended their "Open House." Robert increases his sales by permitting builders and designers of new model homes to display and sell his art.

- Susan creates mixed media work of people's homes and family members using collage, paint and digital photography. She developed sales right in her neighborhood by going door-to-door with her work. She scans her neighborhood for "For Sale" signs and approaches the new homeowners with a small, small rough sketch of their house as a welcome gift and tries to sale a finished work of art. She has developed relationships with several residential real estate brokers who notify her of house sales and have commissioned her to execute drawings to use in their sales brochures. Her telephone number is listed on the brochure for inquiries. She has also developed relationships with commercial brokers who lead her to corporate sales.

- Jim holds an "Open Studio" in the fall and spring. His visitors enjoy a behind-the-scenes tour of his workspace. He creates a casual, clean, safe and uncluttered environment in which they can browse through his work. During the year he invites the children in the nearby school to visit with their parents.

- Akiko rents her work to individuals, law firms, medical spaces, restaurants and real estate offices. She offers the renter the option to buy at any time. She also joined other artists and established an art rental association. (If you try to rent your work make sure you have a written contract and that the first installment is substantial enough to cover insurance if the renter does not carry insurance.)

- James uses his work as a tool for bartering. He exchanges his small paintings with the owner of an upscale local restaurant owner. The arrangement is very convenient when he entertains a collector from out of town and wants to pick up the tab. The restaurant also exhibits and sells his work.

- Steven has avoided paying his tax advisor for seven years through bartering. In March, while many other artists are having anxiety attacks, he calmly delivers his documents and receipts to have his documents prepared. His advisor receives a beautiful new painting in exchange for his efforts. (For barter companies, look in the Yellow Pages under Barter and Trade Exchange. There also are web sites that handle bartering. If you engage in barter, remember to follow the appropriate tax rules.)

A successful man is one who can build a firm foundation
with the bricks that others throw at him.
David Brinkley

Poor artist.
You gave away part of your soul when you painted
the picture which you are now trying to dispose of.
Paul Gaughuin

SELLING YOUR ART IN AN EXHIBITION

Have you ever wondered why many successful artists' gallery exhibitions are completely or nearly sold out before the show opens? It wasn't a matter of luck. Hard work brought about those sales long before opening night. Unless you are fortunate to be represented by an established gallery with a solid following, you will need to implement some sales and marketing plans of your own several months ahead of your exhibition.

Many artists come to me for a consultation at the end of their exhibitions and they have nothing to show from the experience except for a pile of bills. You can avoid this. The selling process does not start the day the exhibition opens. Instead, start the marketing and sales activities the day the exhibition date is set. Develop the planning stages and write all of the essential activities and deadlines on your calendar. If you are short on time it is better to have one less work in the exhibition than one less prospective customer. If you want to increase sales, it is better to do fewer shows with efficient sales strategies than many shows with little effort in the sales department.

When you are in charge of your own sales, start selling the work before the exhibition opens by showing prospective collectors photographs of your work, inviting them to the studio, and discussing your exhibition. Some artists offer special pre-exhibition "Open Studio" events to build anticipation and cultivate pre-exhibition sales among their existing collectors. Many art buyers are delighted to see the work of art they own on display with the red dot indicating, "sold" next to it. This red mark of success also helps to encourage others to buy. (If you want to exhibit a piece and don't want to sell it, display it with a red dot next to it and see how much attention this piece gets.)

If you promote your exhibition properly there will be a wave of energy and excitement at the opening. Many sales are likely to occur then, so be prepared. Hire or recruit at least one person who is knowledgeable about your work and has sales experience. While they handle the sales negotiations and paper work, you can concentrate on meeting as many agents, dealers, writers and prospective buyers as possible. Be cordial to everyone who attends the event, but don't waste too much time talking to unqualified buyers. When speaking to prospective buyers keep the conversation focused on your artwork. At the opening collect the names, addresses and phone numbers of qualified leads with notations about which work they were interested in. The day after the opening reception follow up on serious prospects and continue to follow up on prospects during and after the exhibition.

When the exhibition opens don't sit and wait for buyers to walk in off the street. Call as many people as possible and remind them the exhibition is ready for viewing and that you would be delighted to meet them at the exhibition space. Increase traffic by organizing events in the gallery. Invite upscale groups to hold their meetings and receptions in the exhibition space to increase your show's visibility. Organize activities that will attract buyers as well as the press. Arrange "Meet The Artist" events and list them as "free and open to the public" in the local newspapers, radio and TV stations. Invite student classes, charity organizations and other special interest groups to meet you for a discussion about your work or an art demonstration.

Do a little more each day than you think you possibly can.
Lowell Thomas

AFTER THE SALE KEEP THE CUSTOMER HAPPY

Marketing experts claim that it takes five times the effort to acquire new customers than to repeat a sale to an existing customer. They also state 20% of your buyers will produce 80% percent of your sales. So, whenever you make a sale it should mark the beginning of a long, rewarding relationship.

In an article in *Art Business News* Murray Raphel referred to a study reported in the *Harvard Business Review* conducted by Xerox. The study of nearly half a million people reported if customers were "very satisfied" they would be six times more likely to buy again than if they were only "satisfied."

How do you keep your customers "very satisfied"? Start by going the extra mile during the sale. Offer to deliver and hang the work personally. This could lead to another sale. Give the buyer a bonus, such as a collection of your cards, a list of tips for caring for your work or a coupon on the purchase of their next piece. They won't forget you. Offer them a referral to a good framer or insurance company. They will appreciate your service.

Keep in touch with buyers of your work. A month after a sale, ask them how they are enjoying the acquisition. Continuously increase the customer's perception of the value of your work. Tell them about your awards, exhibitions and other accomplishments. They will probably tell their friends about the wise investment they made, which will lead to more sales and opportunities. Send them visuals of new works. Let them know that you are always creating something new for them to enjoy! Maybe the person who bought a small print is now ready to upgrade to an original painting. Perhaps the owners of your work would purchase one of your works for someone on their gift list. Offer them a variety of price ranges – from note cards to silk-screened T-shirts to prints to originals. Reach out to them through holiday cards that feature your work.

It is important to stay connected for another reason. Before you release your work, you may want to ask the buyer to allow you to borrow the work back for brief periods for important exhibitions. Also agree to get resale information, should they decide to transfer the work to another owner. Agree to a royalty on re-transfer of artwork. Get these agreements in writing!

Writing is easy. All you have to do is stare at a blank sheet of paper until drops of blood form on your forehead.
Gene Fowler

THE ARTIST'S NEWSLETTER

This promotional tool is an excellent way for artists to stay in touch with current and prospective buyers. It can consist of a single sheet or several pages in print or by e-mail. Carole Davis creates a simple "Update", which lists her monthly activities. Anthony Whelihan sends "The Word on Whelihan", which contains photographs of his art and his collectors. Gaye Elise Beda mails an "End of the Year Wrap-Up" which summarizes her annual achievements. Well-known sculptor Carole A. Feuerman produces "Feuerman Studios" that promotes her activities, sells her sculpture and her book and contains a convenient order form.

Don't let writer's block prevent you from using this wonderful sales tool. Keep it simple and let your images do the selling. If you can't write well ask a professional to help you.

CHAPTER 10

RAISING THE VOLUME ON SELF-PROMOTION

Some are born great, others achieve greatness,
and some hire public relations officers.
Daniel J. Boorstein

Perhaps you have never thought about your reputation or how the public perceives you. But, did you know that if you were to raise the volume on self-promotion just a notch you would be amazed at the results you would achieve?

Public Relations is a broad umbrella under which community relations, networking, publicity and a multitude of other activities fall. It is not a new concept. The use of public relations in the arts goes back to Futurism, born in the years immediately preceding World War I. This art movement aimed to agitate an uneasy self-consciousness, and it incorporated advanced techniques of publicity and showmanship. Since then many artists have engaged the services of public relations specialists and self-promotion to advance their careers. For instance, Jackson Pollock and Jacob Epstein shared the same public relations agent, Eleanor Lambert, who specialized in promoting artists' careers.

Public relations is a multi-billion dollar industry. Most experts would agree that nothing in the media today is generated independent of the assistance provided by someone engaged in public relations. The process can begin with a single phone call. The vehicle that drives the message is the news release that is dependent upon excellent writing skills and the packaging of information that tells the merits of the individual, organization, product, event or service. Once disseminated to the correct media outlets it can be shared with the public. Successful public relations is consistent and aggressive and relies on knowing to whom to direct the message.

To get the word out you can use advertising, which can cost a lot of money, or publicity, which does not cost a penny (unless you hire a publicist). In his desire to attain fame and fortune Jeff Koons spared no expense; he bought advertising space in art magazines and billboard space around New York City. Lynda Benglis bought a two-page spread to spread her nude body in *Artforum*, and painter Marilyn Minter bought TV time to announce her exhibit. They did it unabashedly.

Artists who crave the spotlight often develop a talent to attract attention and become popular figures in the art world. Peter Max is an artist whose ambitious public relations and marketing efforts have resulted in making him as the official artist for five Grammy Awards, four Super Bowls, the U.S. Tournament and many other international events and appearing on public television. The late Andy Warhol, who claimed everyone would be famous for fifteen minutes was considered a self-promotion genius. He knew many ways to make himself noticed including wearing a shocking white wig. Keith Haring gained acclaim when he went public with his art in the New York City subways. He made his mark on the walls underground, attracting the attention of thousands of commuters and the evening news.

The definition of "fame" is quite personal. While some artists choose to attract attention by being politically controversial and living unconventional lifestyles other artists prefer to take a more serious, quieter route as they steadily strengthen their careers through critical reviews, fellowships, grants and awards.

You don't need to advertise or hire a public relations firm in order to get the word out about your artistic endeavors. This chapter offers a variety of promotion strategies and advice from experts on how to attract the press. In addition to this chapter review the chapter "Relationships Build Your Power Base." You will also find advice, step-by-step instructions, samples of press releases and other promotional documents and advice from public relations experts in the book *Presentation Power Tools For Fine Artists*. (There is an order form in this book.)

> *To see one's name in print!*
> *Some people commit a crime for no other reason.*
> Gustave Flaubert

SELF-PROMOTION STRATEGIES

- Christian gains popularity by using "cross-promotion." His favorite restaurant hangs his work and features it on their menu. To reciprocate Christian gives each buyer of his work a gift certificate to be redeemed in the restaurant.
- The Richmond Galleries in Marblehead, OH organized a "Breakfast with the Artists" promotion series. They offered a free continental breakfast and gifts and invited guests to meet a different guest artist each month at the gallery.

- Several galleries in New York's Meat Market District drew crowds by promoting "Meat Market Crawls." They all stayed open late on Thursday nights.
- To promote her exhibit Lucia approached galleries nearby and suggested they share expenses for a cooperative flier and advertisement.
- Dennis makes profitable promotional materials by printing his images on T-shirts, canvas bags, note cards and magnets.
- Many artists present talks and slide presentations in schools, museums, civic groups, Chambers of Commerce, Rotary Clubs, church groups, political groups and other institutions. If you do this, photograph and/or record the occasion so you'll be able to propose the idea to other venues.
- An artist caught the attention of a *New York Newsday* writer when he posted thousands of signs and stickers depicting his artwork throughout New York City's subways and phone booths.
- A savvy artist approached an owner of a vacant street level space in SoHo and asked to exhibit her work in it until it was rented. She attracted so much attention for her idea that *The New York Times* gave her full-page coverage.
- Be a big fish in a small pond especially if you live in a small town. If you earn an award or other achievement from an art organization in a major city, use it to boost your name in your hometown. Lynne, an artist living in a small town in California, became a local star. When she was featured in *Manhattan Arts International* magazine she organized a "magazine signing" and exhibition at her local bookstore.
- Be creative when titling your exhibition. Words are important in self-promotion and sales. Until your name alone with "New Works" can draw throngs of people try to choose descriptive titles. A few good examples I have seen are:

"Touch Me Please: Sculpture"; "A Singular Humanity: Figures in Oil"; "Earth Watch: Environmental Mixed Media; and "Mythic Heads and Forms: Paintings." This advice can also be applied to titling your works. Substitute "Untitled 1" or "Untitled 2" with more creative titles and you'll see the difference.

> *In the future everyone will be famous*
> *for fifteen minutes.*
> Andy Warhol

DEALING WITH THE PRESS

You can make more people aware of you and your work by attracting publicity in the form of print, radio, TV or the Internet. This form of exposure will gain the attention of the public, galleries, collectors, grant-givers and critics. As your reputation grows, so does the perceived value of your work.

There are many venues in which to receive publicity. Your press list should contain such categories as daily and weekly newspapers, local news bureaus, bureau offices of national media, monthly newspapers, art publications, wire services, web sites, specialty publications, foreign language publications and periodicals, social press, freelance writers and radio and television stations. *Bacon's Newspaper/Magazine Directory, Editor and Publisher International Yearbook* and *Literary Market Place* are comprehensive resources that list magazines, newspapers, and radio and TV stations and proper contact names and addresses. They can be found in your library. *Also see Appendix II.*

In the beginning, your press list will just be a collection of names, but once you familiarize yourself with the writers and their needs, you will establish relationships with them. It will help you to help them do their job by doing the following:

- Know the deadlines and send materials in time to meet them.
- Mail press releases that they can use in their entirety.
- Write "Contact: (followed by your name and telephone number and e-mail address) at the top of the press release.
- Send attractive visual materials.
- Have printed information ready and available for sending by fax and e-mail.
- Be cordial, professional and polite. Return calls promptly. Send a thank you letter to writers who include you in a review or article, no matter how much "ink" you received.
- Send information to the right people. Keep your press list updated. Make phone calls periodically to confirm if the individuals are still there or if there have been changes in positions.

Your publicity materials will include your press release, black and white and/or color photographs, your biography and/or résumé and a quick fact sheet that lists *Who, What, When, Where* and *Why*. Assemble them in a folder known as a press kit.

Pay attention to every detail, including the quality of the letterhead, the type style and size, the clarity of your message and the neatness of the overall package. If any part of it appears unkempt or incomplete, the recipient may lose interest.

Send the best visuals possible. Edward Rubin has been a writer for over thirty years. His articles have appeared in the *ARTnews, Manhattan Arts International* and *Theatre Week*. He offers this advice: "Artists should send a color reproduction of their work with the press release. I want to get a visual idea of what the art looks like when I receive press materials." In addition to photographs of your work action photographs also grab attention – whether it's of you carving marble, or climbing the mountain to get the perfect photograph, or conducting an art therapy workshop in a hospice.

> *There's only one thing in the world*
> *worse than being talked about,*
> *and that is not being talked about.*
> Oscar Wilde

LEARN FROM PUBLIC RELATIONS EXPERTS

ADVICE FROM JANET APPEL

Janet Appel is President of Janet Appel Public Relations, in New York, NY, and also works as a freelance publicist. She has worked with artists and arts organizations, as well as handled financial, equine, entertainment, fashion and medical-related clients. Janet is very successful because she takes a broad and creative approach in obtaining publicity for her clients. She is also relentless in her efforts. Janet offers this sage advice: "Think outside the box, where you or your work may relate to the publication. It takes time and creative thinking to obtain publicity, and for those who think creatively, the chances are greater."

Janet believes in diversification and encourages artists to look outside the art columns for publicity. "There are usually several ideas that can be generated to create a buzz about the work, or the artist who created it, or perhaps even the location in which it was created." She adds, "There are often several editors or writers to approach particularly on a large publication. Aside from the art world media, there may be others depending on the subject matter of what you do or that your work relates to. For example, if you paint flowers, contact the horticultural non-profit organizations. They might consider featuring you in their newsletter or on their website or in an exhibition."

Janet also believes artists may be overlooking strong possibilities that are quite accessible and says: "Go to some of the smaller publications that are local, for example, where you grew up, your college newspaper, or the alumni association. There are many different media outlets that might just be interested in what you are doing because of a past or current relationship."

When calling the press Janet recommends these tips: "Rehearse your pitch to the media and make sure you can present what you have to say in a clear, concise manner. Be prepared to switch your game plan if your pitch is rejected."

ADVICE FROM CORNELIA SECKEL

Cornelia Seckel is publisher of *Art Times*, a publication founded in 1984 that serves the cultural corridor of the Northeast and provides commentary and resources for all the arts. When she is asked to provide some advice about getting the attention of the media, Cornelia says: "There are several critical things to keep in mind when approaching the media. Among them are: Know the publications/media – their purpose and needs. This means read several issues / listen to broadcasts/view programs. Find out who the people are that you should be contacting – and spelling does count so ask for proper spelling! Ask directly how and when they want information, what specifically they want (statement, pictures, calendar information, etc.), and how the information should be sent – by e-mail or by regular mail. Rarely will someone take information over the phone."

ADVICE FROM
CAROLE SORELL AND JOHN ROSS

Established in 1980, Carole Sorell Incorporated is a public relations firm located in New York, NY, that specializes in the promotion and marketing of the arts and culture. Its principals Carole Sorell and John Ross have extensive experience working with museums, galleries and artists.

Carole and John suggest: "Anything that falls in the art world is considered soft news by the media. There is no reason to write about it unless it is interesting in some way. If you have come up with an unusual idea or concept, you will have a better chance to have it published. Think about what you are publicizing from a journalist's point of view, rather than your own. Present your material in a straight-forward manner. Tact and delicacy is important. Pestering doesn't work and it can alienate the media. If you can swing it – hiring a professional public relations consultant with a background in the arts is a good idea."

PUBLICITY STRATEGIES

- **Suggest a story idea.** Offer the press to write on a subject you know well. If you live in a small community, offer to be the art reporter. If you live in a large city, cover the section of the city about which you are most familiar. Also, many trade publications welcome contributors with knowledge.
- **Write "Letters to the Editor".** When you feel the impulse take action. Make sure that your name and all other pertinent biographical information is added. If they run your article, you may be considered an expert and receive a surge of credibility.

- **Look for angles.** Don't wait for an exhibition to turn the wheels of publicity. Did you recently retire as a dentist to become a full-time artist? Did you win an important award or grant? Did you finish an unusual commission? Is your work controversial or related to current events?

- **"Piggyback" your event with others.** Look for national campaigns and events that relate to you, your work's content and subject matter. For example, October: Breast Cancer Awareness; February: Black History Month; March: Women's History Month; and Earth Day is April 22.

- **Ask for "Editorial Calendars".** You favorite publications can tell you the best time to submit materials. For example, *Manhattan Arts International* presents "The Healing Power of Art" every spring and we feature "Herstory" every March, and we are always looking for good stories.

- **Join forces.** Coordinate your efforts with highly recognized groups and you'll receive huge benefits. As Editor-in-Chief of *Manhattan Arts International* magazine I have hosted many events to promote the Arts. We presented "Salute to French Art and Culture", Salute to Greek Art and Culture" and "Salute to Italian Art and Culture", in which we joined forces with the respective consulates and art groups. We also hosted an exhibition of Ken Duncan's photographs in a New York City gallery – to raise money for the Performing Arts Center for Health. To celebrate American Music Week our magazine organized a "Salute to American Music Week" gala in a New York City club. Special guests consisted of music personalities of all styles, including Beverly Sills, Wynton Marsalis and Frank Zappa, accept *Manhattan Arts* American Music Awards. The event attracted thousands of attendees and received national television, radio and print coverage. We organized the first Manhattan Arts political debate among Manhattan's candidates for Borough President and asked Tony Randall to moderate. Leaders from all disciplines of the Arts and the press were in attendance. The event brought attention to important issues facing the Arts and it placed the magazine in front of a large influential audience.

You can get funding for your event from the public relations departments of companies that in return receive publicity.

No act of kindness, no matter how small,
is ever wasted.
Aesop

RAISE YOUR VOICE AS A VOLUNTEER

Who you are is reflected by the charities you support. Tremendous personal benefits await the volunteer. To bring positive change to someone's life and to be productive in our society, one must make time for meaningful pursuits – to help heal the world in the damaged places. Don't wait until you are wealthy. Small contributions given with the right spirit have great value.

As a young artist, living in the suburbs, I gave free lectures and drawing lessons to children at the local library, organized art fund-raising events for the Chamber of Commerce, and conducted creative discussion groups for patients at a psychiatric hospital. Those formative years helped me to develop confidence, experience and personal satisfaction. Volunteerism has continued to offer me a chance to contribute to worthy causes as well as provide surprising benefits in building relationships and advancing my career. When I arrived in New York City I turned to volunteering as a way of meeting important art leaders and building my résumé. I organized art exhibitions in community centers and banks, wrote art reviews in local community newspapers, served on the Board of Directors of New York Artist's Equity and the panel of jurors on the Awards of Excellence in the Arts for the mayor. Today, I enjoy being a consultant and Vice-President of Artists Advocacy for the Women's Studio Center, a non-profit organization. I frequently conduct free portfolio reviews and workshops to help artists and I donate my books and services to organizations for their fund-raising events. Volunteer work will always be an integral part of my personal life and business.

When we grow old, there can only be one regret –
not to have given enough of ourselves.
Eleanora Duse

Look for opportunities to be generous. You will not only gain satisfaction by helping others, you will also create a positive self-image. Follow your heart, passion and concerns, and you will be led to special interest groups that share your interests. The options are endless – environment, politics, anti-censorship, health care, seniors, Pro-life vs Pro-choice, anti-drugs – to name a few. Volunteer to help in hospitals, libraries, museums, the city council, variety club, United Way, animal protection groups, political clubs, neighborhood improvement groups, girl scouts and religious and cultural groups. Find leads through the Better Business Bureau, Chamber of Commerce, small business clubs, breakfast clubs, business associations and your neighborhood improvement groups.

Don't wait for a charity to approach you. Contact them with an idea. Share your creativity and talent in ways that are useful to the organizations' efforts to raise funds. Offer your art as a vehicle to help them communicate their mission.

If you want to lift yourself up,
lift up someone else.
Booker T. Washington

EXAMPLES OF ARTISTS WHO ARE VOLUNTEERS

These artists who have found a way to channel their creative talent into volunteerism:

- Nadia is a wildlife artist who contributes her images to many regional and national organizations, whose aims are to help save our planet, and raise public awareness.
- Jim, a sculptor, offered a special fund-raising exhibition to an organization for the blind. It was a rewarding experience for him to share his art that the blind could *see* with their hands!
- Boris created the poster for a high profile celebrity AIDS auction, which they sold as a limited edition print. In addition to the recognition he received, he immediately added a number of celebrities to his list of collectors!
- Carlos contributes his time and talent to a children's hospital in Kentucky. His drawings have been reproduced on note cards and posters that have helped to raise funds for the clinic. The exposure he has received has led to exhibitions and sales.

*We can't help everyone,
but everyone can help someone.*
Dr. Loretta Scott

- Yuriko gives proceeds from sales in her exhibitions to different local charities. In appreciation the charity publishes news of her generosity of spirit in their bulletin and sends out press releases on her behalf.
- Rolf's brightly-colored paintings depict social concerns in a whimsical style. He approached the Arthur Ashe Foundation directly and they used his images on T-shirts and posters, which received world-wide exposure.
- Nancy, a recent graduate, is a volunteer caricaturist for a senior center. From this activity she gets jobs to do caricatures at the parties of the residents' relatives.
- Mark gives free workshops in his local library, community center and church. The experience has helped to raise his self-confidence and prepared him for taking his talks to larger audiences, such as universities and museums.
- Margarite's weekly visits to see her grandmother in a hospice ignited the idea to brighten the place with healing artwork. She recruited some artist friends to donate art for the hospice's hallways and reception areas. They bring art supplies with them and encourage the patients to create art.
- Delilah volunteers to clean up abandoned public playgrounds in lower income neighborhoods by creating mural art with the local children in an after school program.
- Stephen gives motivational talks to high school art students in their senior year to help them select from different career options after graduation.

CHAPTER 11

WOMEN ARTISTS
MOVING FORWARD

*Historically, women have either been excluded
from the process of creating the definitions of what is
considered art or allowed to participate only if we accept
and work within existing mainstream designations.*
Judy Chicago

For centuries women artists have endured limited artistic options. We have come a long way since Artemisia Gentileschi's time but we must still continue to forge ahead. When I was asked to participate on a panel "The Status of Women in the Arts" sponsored by Women Executives in Public Relations I examined *The Complete Guide To New York Art Galleries* and observed only 30% of the artists represented by New York City galleries were women. I perused *Art in America Guide to Museums, Galleries and Artists* and noticed that major galleries listed four men to one woman in their advertisements. I read Eleanor Dickinson's *STATISTICS: Gender Discrimination in the Art Field*, sent to me by The Archive Dept. of the National Museum of Women in the Arts in Washington, DC, which contains copious data derived from universities, museums, census bureaus, the Bureau of Labor Statistics and other sources. It revealed a shocking disparity between the nation's consensus bureau of women artists and economic equality.

Howardena Pindell says in her book *The Heart of the Question*, "There is a closed circle which links the museums, galleries, auction houses, collectors, critics and art museums which systematically excludes minorities." Why do men far outnumber women in galleries? Why are 70% of the museum shows given to men? Why are women's art in auctions sold at lower prices than men? What can we do to level the playing field?

These questions led me to four dynamic women leaders in the Arts: Joan Arbiter; Eleanor Dickinson; Marcelle Harwell Pachnowski; and Melissa Wolf. I am grateful for the knowledge and experience they contributed to this chapter to see the history of women in the arts through their eyes. Space prevents me from crediting everyone who has made significant contributions to the women's art movement. I apologize to those we omitted.

COMMENTS FROM JOAN ARBEITER

Joan Arbeiter is an artist, art educator and co-author of Lives and Works: Talks with Women Artists. *She received her BA from Brooklyn College and her MFA from Pratt Institute. She directed the Joan Arbeiter Studio School (1976-1988) and joined the faculty of The DuCret School of Art in 1978, where she continues to teach.*

I came to feminist consciousness in the late '70's and early '80's" when I discovered the women's art movement. Until that time, women artists had been largely excluded from the textbooks and museums. Even though we received an "education" in art history at both the undergraduate and graduate levels, we had no idea of what had been left out.

It was a revelation, in 1977, to see the Brooklyn Museum exhibit, "Women Artists 1550-1950," curated by Linda Nochlin and Ann Sutherland Harris. Three years later, also at the

Brooklyn Museum, it was equally thrilling to encounter Judy Chicago's "The Dinner Party," celebrating and documenting one hundred women in history, appeared also at the Brooklyn Museum.

Meantime, The New York Feminist Art Institute opened its doors, and for the next eleven years, under the guidance of Nancy Azara and others, its classes and programs energized and influenced so many of us. It was Nancy's "Visual Diaries" classes that confirmed my personal and political transformation. I became part of the movement, as I worked side by side with Faith Ringgold (making spirit dolls) and Judy Chicago (in her birthing workshop). In 1983 many of us were ready to start our own artist-run gallery, Ceres, and I have been exhibiting there since. I love running the educational programs, especially those in celebration of women's history.

The Women's Caucus for Art (WCA), both national and local, was also a crucial influence on us all. (The WCA grew out of the College Art Association.) I responded eagerly to Judith Brodsky's invitation to help organize our local WCA chapter, which gave us the opportunity to make our presence felt on our own terms. At the national annual conferences there were feminist art history lectures setting the record straight, artists' panels, exhibits, performances, networking, and, especially, awards ceremonies. This recognition for overlooked but incredible women in the arts was a powerful inspiration. We were rescuing our history from oblivion, and each of us became conscious of our own ability to continue to create this history.

Thus in 1988, when I was invited to co-author a book of interviews of contemporary women artists titled *Lives and Works: Talks with Women Artists, Vol. 2* (published by Scarecrow), I was fully aware that I would be contributing to much-needed documentation. What a thrill to introduce both the book and many of its featured artists who came to speak to a large, appreciative audience at the National Museum of Women in the Arts

(NMWA). Additionally, this book generated two exhibits. In the first, I curated a show of these artists' work. The second is my own mixed media series of portraits of these artists, accompanied by text panels. This exhibition has become a traveling educational tool for college art galleries in celebration of Women's History Month.

As the percentage of women exhibiting in galleries and museums increased, the newer generation started to take our hand-won gains for granted. We began to suffer from a loss of new leadership and a decrease in numbers of women exhibiting in solo exhibitions. So when I met Melissa Wolf at a women's art conference at Barnard, and she outlined her plans for the Women's Studio Center, I was overjoyed. I see her as a kind of savior and have helped her to connect with those who have experience and influence. In 2003, I was pleased that Melissa became the program chair for the national WCA conference. Women's history is fragile and needs to be preserved, protected and published.

My life in the arts has been listening, learning, teaching, networking, documenting, mentoring – both given and received, and of course exhibiting. As a lovely bonus, all of this has immeasurably enriched the content of my studio work.

COMMENTS FROM ELEANOR DICKINSON

Eleanor Dickinson is an innovative figure painter, video artist and professor. She has fought for Artists Rights legislation through Artists Equity Association, the Women's Caucus for Art and California Lawyers for the Arts, serving on their Boards. Her work has been shown in 24 solo museum exhibitions including the Corcoran Gallery of Art, Washington, D.C.

In 1971 I started the first US undergraduate course in Professional Practices in art (there was one class for Grad students teaching aesthetics in hanging museum exhibitions at Cal State

Fullerton before that) at the California College of Arts and Crafts (now renamed the California College of the Arts) and it is still being offered. Many colleges and universities now have them. I also started a TV program called "The 'art of the Matter" in the Bay Area on cable TV in 1986 covering the same material and it is still going: people can take this free. It's a godsend for art students who want to survive in a tough world. (The Oakland campus is: 5212 Broadway, Oakland, CA 94618. Telephone: 510-597-3600. The San Francisco campus is 450 Irwin St., San Francisco, CA 94107. Telephone: 415-703-9500.)

We all have heard of the problems of gender discrimination in the Art World today. Although 44% of U.S. artists are women and 53% of the art degrees in the U.S. go to women, only 16% of the artists in Invited Exhibitions are women as compared with 43% of women in exhibitions Juried for excellence alone. There is probably a similar distortion in race and media discrimination. Much of this discrepancy is caused by the bad work habits of the directors and curators who choose the art to be shown in galleries and museums today. Much of this could be remedied by pressure from these art institutions to demand greater involvement in the art community by their staff to avoid the "Old Boy System" and develop an awareness of the incredible, fascinating diversity of both artists and art-making in our country today.

Over the years that we have fought discrimination, however, I have noticed things that make me uneasy: that call for women to share some of the blame for the difference between the availability of accomplished women artists and the low number chosen for exhibitions. Many, many women today are still being brought up to be passive, often by their families before they are even aware of it (I saw my sister-in-law coo to her newborn girl twins, "Don't frown like that! You'll never get a husband that way.")

When their art career does not go well, when they notice male artists' careers are flourishing while their un-shown, unsold art piles up in the garage they turn their anger, frustration and hatred in upon themselves – feel that it is their own inadequacy – instead of turning that anger to proper use in combating the discrimination.

An ardent feminist, my former student, became Director of a good University gallery. She was determined to show at least one-half women. In two years the best she could do was to show one-third women with a great deal of extra work on her part. There was no problem with the quality of the artwork or the number of women artists available and eager to show. She was constantly plagued by the lack of basic professional behavior. Slides were badly done, poorly labeled, no lists made; frames were inadequate or absent, résumés not done, calls not returned. The women expected that all the work would be done for them: framing, listing, transporting work to the gallery, the mailing, raising grant money, insurance, returning the art. When she showed a male artist, however, he would show up with his buddies to help; the women would not.

Many women artists are not doing their homework so that they will be prepared for the opportunities they have or could make. There is a great lack of professionalism. An artist must be prepared to do all the hard work and must have the knowledge to do it well. They must take every class they can in Professional Practices: art law, contracts, copyrights, packing and shipping, insurance, photography, graphic design, portfolios, exhibition design and lighting – everything.

An artist knows that she may not succeed: that it is a lifelong struggle for financial support, for aesthetic understanding and for honesty in her work. She needs to have everything professional going for her so that she will do excellent work and also have the world know it!

COMMENTS FROM
MARCELLE HARWELL PACHNOWSKI

Marcelle Harwell Pachnowski is an artist and former President of the National Association of Women Artists (NAWA). She holds her MFA in painting and drawing from the University of Maryland and her BA from the American University in Washington, D.C. She has had exhibitions on national and international levels and her work is in numerous collections. She has taught at the University of Maryland, Western Carolina University, Columbus College, Duke Ellington School of the Arts in Washington, D.C., Baltimore School of the Arts and Gibbes Museum School in Charleston, to name a few.

When I lived in a small community in the mountains of North Carolina I negotiated with county and state officials to start an arts council. We successfully organized many fundraisers, art festivals and regularly brought artists-in-residence to their public schools. When I lived in Atlanta, Georgia I was an artist-in-residence on the city, county and state levels that were funded by local arts councils, the Georgia Council for the Arts and the National Endowment for the Arts. While living in Atlanta, I was the first visual artist to be involved in an artist-residence in a homeless shelter for women and children. I also lobbied for art advocacy in Atlanta.

As President of NAWA, I supported our mission of promoting women artists by women artists, secured accredited national venues, established internship programs with universities and art schools, offered professional development opportunities and pursued grant funding. NAWA is the oldest and largest exhibiting organization of women artists that dates back to 1889 with such members as Mary Cassatt, Suzanne Valadon, Louise Nevelson, Marisol and Judy Chicago, to name a few. It currently has 800 members. The Zimmerli Art Museum at Rutgers University holds a permanent collection of NAWA members.

When NAWA received a grant from the Rockefeller Foundation (Blanchette Hooker Foundation), which was disbursed during a three-year period, we realized we needed to take measures to raise the organization's recognition and take care of business. We saw the need to restructure the organization and subsequently created an Artists Council, consisting of artist members, in addition to a Governing Board, consisting of a variety of professional men and women such as an attorney, fund-raiser, development specialist, financial advisor and a museum director. We learned the importance of implementing outreach programs and we have brought art programs to a community hospital.

My advice to women artists:

- Never bi-pass a "business of art" class. Take it!
- Learn to keep accurate records (have contact with an accountant).
- Be aware of legal issues for artists such as contracts and copyrights (have contact with an attorney).
- Don't be shy of writing. Don't say to yourself, "I'm an artist, I'm visual, I don't have to be verbal". Wrong. Be articulate.
- Be computer literate.
- Network with the curator, the dealer, the collector, the art critic.

COMMENTS FROM MELISSA WOLF

Melissa Wolf is Executive Director of the Women's Studio Center, a fine arts studio in Long Island City, NY that offers studio space, classes, workshops, programs, exhibitions, literary readings and events for Visual Artists and Writers. It is also a resource center that provides information about women in the arts to artists, the art world and the general public. Melissa has a certificate in Arts Administration from NYU and is a member of ArtTable. She is a non-practicing artist.

The good news is that we are on the cusp of significant change for women artists. There is a wider fascination developing with women artists. Museums are having more blockbuster exhibitions than ever before like Artemesia Gentileschi's exhibition at the Metropolitan Museum and Frida Kahlo's exhibition which attracted an unprecedented number of visitors to El Museo del Barrio. Another significant stride was Elizabeth A. Sackler's gifting of Judy Chicago's "The Dinner Party" to the Brooklyn Museum of Art where it is on permanent display in the Elizabeth A. Sackler wing.

It is important to try to build relationships among the organization's members and between the organization and the community. We are focused on getting the artist ready for the market and bringing the market to the artist. As the managing editor of *Women's Arts News,* a publication highlighting history and current events of women in the arts, I find more and more galleries and museums seeking us out to publicize their exhibitions. We need to ride this wave, to take this significant moment to encourage the number of women artists out there. Now, more than ever, creating change is about creating relationships and doing business. Creating change is about our personal success.

As individuals, as artists and as women, we need to teach ourselves about business. We need to seek out organizations that exclusively support and educate women in areas of finance, general business practices – such as marketing, networking and entrepreneurship. These organizations include the National Association of Female Executives (NAFE), Women and Company (a division of Citibank), and the American Women's Economic Development Corporation. Even Senior Core of Retired Executives (SCORE), a service where retired executives give business advice to business owners, has a women specific division. There are probably even more community-based organizations in your area. NAFE and Women and Company have chapters. Be an active, vocal part of these organizations and let them know that artists serve the community and make use of services in their community as well. As each one of us becomes successful we begin to make a difference just by existing and by being visible.

I became an artist for the same reason
I became a writer – I wanted to tell my story.
Faith Ringgold

SUPPORT FOR WOMEN ARTISTS

At the forefront of supportive institutions is The National Museum of Women in the Arts (NMWA) in Washington, DC whose mission is, "To bring recognition to the achievements of women artists of all periods and nationalities by exhibiting, preserving, acquiring and researching art by women and by educating the public concerning their accomplishments." Its permanent collection, with more than 3,000 works, provides a comprehensive survey of art by women from the 16th century to the present.

There are many organizations, foundations and galleries that are playing an important role in leveling the playing field in the art world. Anonymous Was A Woman was established in response to the elimination of fellowships by the NEA. Guerrilla Girls in New York City and California have made positive changes through public exposure and protests.

Still in existence and going strong are many of the galleries that were established in the '70's to give women artists representation and to show art with materials and subject matter that were not accepted by commercial galleries including ARC Gallery, started in 1973 in Chicago. Run by women the gallery also shows the work of men artists. In the summer of 2003 there was a panel discussion in celebration of ARC's 30th anniversary. In reporting the event in *The Chicago Artists' News* writer Judy Prisoc quoted Aimee Picard, board member of Woman Made Gallery in Chicago as saying although there used to be an Old Boys Network, "We have created our own networks..." Aimee added, "But, we need to keep breaking down the walls that keep us from participating."

New York City is also the home of several galleries that are run by women artists. Located in Chelsea, the mecca of galleries in Manhattan, we have AIR, Ceres and SoHo 20. There are also many women's arts organizations in New York City including The Crystal Quilt, Guerrilla Girls, National Association of Women Artists, New York Society of Women Artists, Pen & Brush Club, Professional Women Photographers, Women's Studio Center and Catharine Lorillard Wolfe Art Club. *(See Appendix II for artists' organizations.)*

We never know how high we are till we are called to rise.
And then, if we are true to plan our statures touch the skies.
Emily Dickinson

WOMEN GAINING POWER

I strongly believe that women will have equal power when their net worth equals their self worth. The commercial art world is a business and money rules. Education is the path to equality. I also believe that we must never allow ourselves to be blinded by selfish ambition that we turn out backs on each other. When Dr. Elizabeth A. Sackler gifted Judy Chicago's "The Dinner Party" to the Brooklyn Museum she was awarded the first Women in the Arts award for her "scholarly contribution, vision and generous patronage." In her acceptance speech she referred to how she was raised and said, "I was told, quite frequently, that one must leave the world a better place than when one arrives... It is my sincerest hope that my gift to this museum supports and makes home for women in the arts who hold justice, equality and peace as primary tenets of goals to be achieved."

MORE ADVICE FOR WOMEN ARTISTS

- Continue to network among yourselves and increase your practice of networking with men.
- Sharpen your business, financial management and wealth-building skills.
- Be assertive and visible in the art community and the world at large.
- Learn to delegate. Become your own CEO.
- Keep your eye on the big picture, not the minutia.

Those of us who want to help women artists can:
- Make a conscious commitment to buy more women artists' work.
- Contribute time and money to help women artists' organizations.
- Place women's artwork in major auctions to increase the value of their art.
- Recommend, hire and support qualified women for jobs in fine art institutions.
- Volunteer to help women artists, women arts organizations and women art galleries. Serve on their advisory boards.
- Become a mentor for women artists.
- Write and speak about the discrimination that exists against women and all minorities.

CHAPTER 12

ARE JURIED COMPETITIONS
WORTH THE GAMBLE?

At last I could work with complete independence
without concerning myself with the eventual judgment of a jury...
I began to live.
Mary Cassatt (Her statement after the Salon rejected her painting.)

C ompetitions that are juried by art critics and museum curators are viewed by many artists as opportunities to have their work juried by respected professionals for career advancement, and as ways to increase exposure, sales and awards. If they take place in notable museums and art councils they are considered more prestigious than many commercial galleries. For artists who have yet to acquire gallery representation, juried shows may serve as their only venues for exposure. Many dealers discover new talent in them and from reading the reviews by critics who write about them. And, having honors and awards obtained from juried shows may gain the attention and respect of collectors and members of the art community.

Competitions that produce catalogues, present purchase and cash awards, and other prizes are difficult to resist. However, as appealing as juried competitions may be, even the best competitions reward only the few.

There are several publications and web sites that list competitions including: *Art in America, American Artist, Art Calendar,* www.ArtDeadlinesList.com, www.Artdeadline.com and www.ManhattanArts.com. *(See Appendix II.)*

A TOSS OF THE DICE

The average entry fee for juried competitions is $25.00. For many struggling non-profit organizations and artist-run galleries, the income derived from competitions helps to offset their annual expenses. Many artists are adamantly opposed to juried exhibitions, especially those with entry fees, and dismiss them as a waste of time and money. They may say luck or politics – not skill – determines the outcome. An artist who wins a top prize in one competition may be rejected in another with the same entry. A reason may be that the second competition may have attracted artists of a higher caliber making the competition tougher, but the truth is, the process of judging work is far from an exact science. Jurors try to be objective but everyone has their own preferences. My experience as a juror on many panels has educated me about the tastes of different jurors. We don't always agree on what deserves merit.

American Artist magazine is one of the most comprehensive sources for competition listings. According to its Editor-in-Chief M. Stephen Doherty: "Competitions offer some good news and some bad news. The good news is, ultimately, the competitions are based on quality alone. Artists who live in Belgium and South Africa are offered an equal opportunity to receive recognition with artists who live in major cities in the U.S. However, each year there are tougher competitors. The number of entries increase." He added: "Often the ultimate decisions by the judges are somewhat arbitrary and several hundred artists may have to be thrown out simply because there is no space."

Although the objective is to win, many artists feel competitions are worth entering, even if they don't win, because the esteemed judges will become acquainted with their work. Gallery 84, a former New York City gallery, attracted nearly 1,000 entries and 4,000 slides one year to its Annual Competition. Gallery Director Joe Bascom attributed the overwhelming response to having chosen Donald Kuspit, a prominent art critic as the juror, and the gallery's prestigious 57 Street location. The competition selected only twenty-five winners – about 2-1/2% of the entries. These figures are representative of most major city exhibitions judged by major critics and museum curators. High tolerance to rejection is required when entering competitions. If an artist relies on competitions to monitor their success or failure as an artist, they will be setting themselves up for disappointment.

COMPETITIONS LEVEL THE PLAYING FIELD

Juried exhibitions in non-profit venues offer what many commercial galleries do not – a level playing field. Artists are judged on the merit of their work alone. That's good news to women and other minority artists, young artists starting out, and more mature artists who may be restarting their careers. New York Artists Equity Association held a competition that was juried by Geno Rodriguez, Director of the Alternative Museum, in New York City. It attracted 800 artists from around the country. 55% of the entrants were women. Unaware of the gender of the entrants, Rodriguez selected 29 artists, of which 21 were women. Several years ago, Pernod (producer of the French aperitif), held an open competition, with four judges from the New York City art community, including Robert Storr, curator of Contemporary Painting and Sculpture at the Museum of Modern Art, and art critic Carlo McCormick. The rules specifically announced: "Open to any artist who has not had a one-person show at an 'established' or 'professional gallery'." There was no entry fee. The first-place winner received $5,000 and a group exhibition in a New York City gallery, with nine additional winners. More than 2,300 works of art were entered by 300 artists. This not only helped many emerging artists it also made great business sense for Pernod by generating positive publicity for their products. It is a practice that should be followed more often by businesses.

ARTISTS BEWARE

Competitions can serve as quick and easy profits for unscrupulous organizations. You may recall the New England Fine Art Institute's "State of the Art '93" juried competition. An estimated number of 2,600 artists paid a minimum of $25 to enter, and if their work was selected there was an additional $49 hanging fee. The artists who attended the exhibition saw that many of the artworks remained in their crates and were never exhibited. The "Institute" was revealed to be, in fact, a small, temporary, rented office space. Numerous complaints were made to the Complaint Division of the Eastern Massachusetts Better Business Bureau and to George K. Weber, Assistant Attorney General, Commonwealth of Massachusetts.

When you learn about similar practices you should make formal complaints. And, try to avoid them by looking for these warnings signs:

- The prospectus is unprofessionally written and/or poorly printed.

- The telephone number is not listed.
- A post office box is supplied for an unknown institution.
- The names of the jurors are not stated or they do not have professional credentials.
- When contacted the organizers will not supply satisfactory information about previous competition entries, winners and cash prizes.
- In addition to the entry fee there are hanging fees and other expenses.

If the material appears to look professional but the organization is unknown, you should still be prepared to research the organization and ask for references. Check the Better Business Bureau, Chamber of Commerce, Attorney General's Office and regional and national arts organizations. If the sponsor claims to be a foundation, check The Foundation Center, in NYC. *(See Appendix II.)* Share your suspicions and information with other artists, professional art organizations and art publications that expose fraudulent practices, such as *Art Calendar,* New York Artists Equity Association and www.ManhattanArts.com.

WAYS TO INCREASE YOUR SUCCESS

- Submit your best work. When selecting slides, remember that in most situations your work has less than one minute to make an impact. One gallery reported a major art critic took only two hours to view a few hundred slides. In another New York City competition the judge took less than an eight-hour day to view 1,000 slides.
- Do your homework. Before you decide to enter the competition learn about the tastes of the jurors, such as what exhibitions they have curated or written about. If the juror is

known to be very partial toward a specific style (not yours) perhaps you would have a better chance elsewhere.

- Find out if possible what is important to the judges. Many judges, like myself, seek technical prowess and innovation. When Nancy di Benedetto, art historian and educator juried the Manhattan Arts International 20th Anniversary competition she said: "The finalists were selected on the basis of three criteria: innovative conceptual perception, unique personal expression and mastery of the medium."

- When making your selection, be objective, and ask: Are you entering your best work? Does it have technical flaws? Is your entry ordinary or innovative? Does your work evoke a strong reaction? Does the composition, design and subject matter attract the viewer's attention and retain their interest?

- If the competition requires judging from original works of art, pay attention to proper matting, framing, and packaging.

- Follow every instruction outlined in the prospectus.

- Make sure your slides or photographic entries are the best quality possible. Don't submit slides that are out of focus, with scratches, glare, or distracting objects. View the slides in a projector before submitting them. Make sure the slide mount isn't warped. Label your slides correctly, according to the specifications outlined on the prospectus. Use adhesive labels that will not fall off when subjected to the heat of the projector. Label your slides with non-smearing ink.

- Use plastic sleeves; don't throw the slides loosely into an envelope. Mail the slides with protective padding.

- Unless another size is requested enclose a business-sized (4 1/8" x 9-1/2") self-addressed, postage-paid envelope with the proper amount of postage, for the return of your slides.

CHAPTER 13

REJECTION IS
A MATTER OF PERSPECTIVE

I was taught that the way of progress
is neither swift nor easy.
Marie Curie

As you make strides to advance your professional status, rejection will tap on your door periodically as a test of your convictions. The higher you set the bar, the harder the fall. Rejection may cause you excruciating pain and remorse. It may even temporarily cause creative paralysis. The fear of criticism and rejection discourages many artists from stretching themselves and testing new grounds in the artistic, financial and career areas of their lives. They may set only a few minor goals or none at all. They may turn their fears into defensive and aggressive behavior and attack others with criticism and rejection.

Criticism and rejection can serve as sources of powerful transformation. Examine your reactions to rejection and you'll find the tools to expand your education, personal growth and humility. To shield you from emotional destruction build a fortress constructed with a positive attitude, confidence, passion and persistence.

Results! I have gotten thousands of results.
I know several thousand things that won't work.

Thomas A. Edison

Len, who is an optimistic and proactive artist, submitted unsolicited materials to a New York City gallery. He thought his work was appropriate for them but, to his dismay, the owner returned his slides with a polite rejection letter. Len's confidence in his work kept him moving forward and he continued to send out his slides to galleries and juried competitions. A few months later he received a letter of acceptance into a competition judged by Klaus Kertess, which awarded him a group exhibition in a New York City gallery. On a whim, he sent the same slides to the dealer who rejected him and in his cover letter he extended an invitation to her to attend his opening reception. Within two weeks, he received a call from her and an invitation to be included in a future group exhibition at her gallery.

Did the dealer's perception of Len's work change after learning about the competition judged by Klaus Kertess? Len may not know the reason but he knows that persistence pays. He knows not to retreat at the first sign of rejection.

Mark Rothko said: "The unfriendliness of society to his (her) activity is difficult for the artist to accept. Yet this very hostility can act as a lever for true liberation." Rejection can serve as a powerful stimulus to creative productivity. Instead of letting rejection tear you apart transform the emotions into a work of art. It may be among the most satisfying works you have ever created. As an artist you have the ability to express your pain and the process can serve to heal not only yourself but the viewer as well.

"Don't judge each day by the harvest you reap,

but by the seeds you sow."

Robert Louis Stevenson

THE IMPORTANCE OF OBJECTIVITY

After you experience a form of rejection or criticism, try to step back and review the events objectively, as though you were watching a movie about someone else, while you ask yourself some questions. At what point did the situation go badly? Did you submit the best quality slides for consideration? Were the decision-makers partial to a style different than yours? Were there politics involved in making the decision? Did your behavior in the interview jeopardize your chances of getting accepted? Did you make a sincere effort to prepare properly? Could you have sent out more proposals to increase your chances of success? Does your exhibition history match those of the other artists who were competing against you? Did you rely on someone else to carry out your responsibilities?

If the causes for receiving a negative reaction to your work are clear, you can avoid repeating the experience. It has been said the only bad experience is one in which you didn't learn anything. However, in many situations, you may never know the reason why your work was rejected. If so, don't waste your energy trying to analyze something you may never understand.

There are many uncontrollable factors that have nothing to do with you or the quality of your work. Rejection is frequently the result of an opinion of one or more individuals. In the final analysis, the only evaluation that should be of real value to you should be your own.

Dollars and Sense

Don't expect every dealer, critic, grant-giver or art buyer to comprehend or respect the heart, soul, feelings and ideas that went into your work. When a dealer rejects your work, there is a very good reason not to be offended. In addition to their personal taste, their decisions may be based more on economics than aesthetics. They must consider whether they have the right clientele for your work, or whether they have time, space or finances to promote a new artist. Keep in mind not all dealers have advanced educational qualifications in Fine Art with which to make an astute judgment about your work.

Even when they do personally admire your work their heart and their bank account may be far apart. Corinne Shane is President of InvestinArt, an art consulting business in New York City, whose clients consist of corporations. When she assisted me in jurying the *Manhattan Arts International* magazine cover competition she made several selections for the magazine but confessed, "Although I personally love this piece, and it deserves an award, it would not be suitable for my corporate clients."

My experience on jurying panels has taught me if you place a diversified group of art critics, collectors and art dealers in a room together with a wide variety of artwork, chances are they will not agree on which shows or artists are the best and the worst. And, they are likely to change their minds during and after the initial discussion.

History has proven that the judgments of "experts" are changeable. Remember, genuine interest in Vincent van Gogh's came after his death. Robert Rauschenberg's first show at Leo Castelli Gallery barely got off the ground. Jean Dubuffet didn't have his first exhibition until he reached the ripe age of

43. Historically, the Whitney Biennials have become the show many critics love to hate. For several years people have claimed that painting is dead, yet we know that is far from true.

If you're not receiving as many acceptances as you would like, examine the methods you are currently using. Review your five-year plan; it may need some changes. Does it still fit your needs? Does it support the changes in the economy? Do you need to search for new alternatives? What useful tactics of successful role models can you apply?

DIVERSIFY TO INCREASE YOUR SUCCESS

A good way to minimize rejection is through diversification. You certainly wouldn't put your entire life's savings into one stock fund. Financial experts advise us to have a "diversified portfolio." The same is true of business success. No single advertising, promotional or marketing strategy works in isolation or indefinitely. Develop exposure through several galleries, competitions, private dealers and grants – on a regional, national and international level. Vary the sizes, media and therefore the prices of your work accordingly. Develop a promotional system that has a steady momentum and routine. Keep your eyes open for new galleries, changes in ownership and leadership, and burgeoning opportunities offered throughout the arts community.

Diversification will not only increase your potential for success it will cushion rejection when it comes: You will be too busy to allow rejection to effect you.

Increase your odds by increasing your activities. Every time you receive a rejection notice, balance the scales by sending out more proposals and making more phone calls, and thereby increasing your chances of receiving positive feedback. Calculate the number of attempts you have to make before you finally sell a work of art or acquire a commission. Divide the selling price by that number. Every time you receive a rejection, say to yourself, "I am 'X' prospects closer to meeting the buyer."

DON'T BURN YOUR BRIDGES

In the face of rejection, be as gracious as possible, safeguard your dignity and ego and don't burn bridges. If one gallery rejects your work, it may not close the door permanently. If you think your work is appropriate for them, try again later. Many events may affect their attitude in the future, such as the director may get fired, their finances may improve, or an artist may leave and create an opening for you. In addition, I have known artists to be rejected by the directors of the galleries only to be contacted by their assistants who opened their *own* galleries.

As tempting as it might be to burn all of your rejection letters, keep them on file with your business records and receipts. According to tax advisors they help prove to the IRS that you are making every attempt to sell your work and that you are not a hobbyist. Then, if you take a loss on Schedule C, you have legitimate proof that you are engaging in professional activities.

Success is simply a matter of luck. Ask any failure.
Earl Wilson

Luck, you may say, is what success is all about. You may believe, "You have to be in the right place at the right time." The truth is, luck is when preparedness meets opportunity. Innate talent, intelligence and years of effort and commitment are needed to become an "overnight" success. Opportunities are everywhere. Be persistent, proactive and plan for success, like these artists:

- Lee is a sculptor who was continuously turned away by galleries until a leading New York City gallery owner saw her work in a doctor's office and asked her to join the gallery.
- Tomas, a painter, tried an alternative route to a gallery and exhibited his work in a bank. He sold several paintings including one to the wife of a major software company.
- Vera, a watercolor artist, takes her slides and sketchbook when she travels. On a trip to Italy she sat next to a serious art collector who bought a drawing from her before they touched ground and became a loyal collector of her work.
- Luis placed his hanging sculpture in a boutique window. A newlywed couple strolled by at night and was so struck by the work glistening in the moonlight they bought the $10,000 piece the following day.
- A New York artist approached a management company that had an empty store for rent and arranged to place her art there until they found a renter. She received free exhibition space and they received a way to attract more people to their available space.

Your attitude will get you through the most difficult times. Remind yourself of your many accomplishments and be proud. Don't dwell on your failures. Don't wallow in self-pity. Try a humorous approach, and write a rejection letter, in which you reject the rejection letter you received, and then tear it up. Smile in the face of rejection and look for the lesson. You may gain more value from an experience than if you hadn't been rejected.

Helen Keller said: "When one door of happiness closes, another opens; but often we look so long at the closed door that we do not see the one which has been opened for us."

THE "O" IN NO STANDS FOR OPPORTUNITY

When you hear the word "no" it often signals the beginning, not the end. It is an opportunity to ask questions and transform rejections into positive responses.

- **Keep calm.** In the face of resistance, avoid the temptation to argue, flee, or compromise your integrity. Instead, say: "I accept your opinion. Can you tell me the reason why?"

- **Explore possibilities.** Try: "I understand the watercolors are not suitable for you at this time, would you like to see my charcoal drawings?"

- **Obtain specific objections.** You might say: "Which aspect are you saying no to – the size, color, or price…?"

- **Show understanding.** Say: "I understand that spending $5,000 is a big consideration. Would you like me to call you next week?" or "Would you like to pay in installments?"

- **Find out who the decision-maker is.** The person may not have the authority to make a decision. You might say: "Would you like to discuss it with your spouse or partner and come back with them?"

- **Try to eliminate fear.** "No" may mask the fear of making the wrong decision. You might say: "May I bring it to your office (or home) to see how it will look?"

- **Stimulate trust and confidence.** Say: "The ABC Corp. recently acquired my work for their lobby and are very satisfied. Would you like to see the letter I received from them?"

- **Assure the buyer that you are a serious artist.** You may say: "I paint everyday… My work has steadily increased in value… I'll have a one-person show in two months."

- **Don't burn your bridges.** Secure the green light to keep in touch. Say: "May I send you an invitation to my next Open Studio?"

CHAPTER 14

EMERGING
AT MATURITY

Old age is not a disease – it is strength and survivorship,
triumph over all kinds of vicissitudes and disappointments,
trials and illnesses.
Maggie Kuhn

For any number of reasons, such as having to work full-time in another field to support yourself and your family or having to be a full-time caregiver to your children you may be facing your career as an "emerging" artist while, chronologically you are in the middle or late stage of your life.

Everyone knows about the primitive artist Grandma Moses (born Anna Mary Roberts) who wasn't serious about painting until she was in her mid 70's. At the age of 79 she had her first one-woman show at Galerie Saint-Etienne in New York. She lived to celebrate her 101st birthday and in the last year of her life she painted 25 works of art. Indeed her story is inspiring, but it is also rare.

We live in a society that is obsessed with youth, and the art world is no exception. The new talent about to be discovered is more likely to be a 25-year-old installation artist than a 65-year-old seasoned veteran. So pervasive is the ambition to be successful at a young age that I have encountered many artists in their late 20's already worrying about not yet being represented by a major gallery. Imagine that! They have high, unrealistic expectations that will head them straight to disappointment.

Few rewards are granted to the mature artist who has mastered his or her medium and created an extensive body of work over more than a decade. In spite of all obstacles you may have persevered as an artist, but your résumé may lack necessary credentials such as exhibitions and honors. Perhaps you have spent more time on creating a solid body of work than luring collectors who have the prestige to propel your career to the cover of *ART-news*. If so, you shouldn't be discouraged. It might be time to retune your career objectives or pick up the pace on self-promotion. Either way, it helps to find inspiration from others.

We don't grow older we grow riper.
Pablo Picasso

THE MASTERS WHO RIPENED WITH AGE

We can first find inspiration from artists who have mastered their art and found commercial success later in life. Agnes Martin, a Canadian-born American painter, was born in 1912. In the late 1930's and the 1940's, she taught in public schools. She was 46 years old when she had her first solo exhibition at the famed Betty Parsons Gallery in New York. In 1973, she had a major retrospective of her work at the Institute of Contemporary Art in Philadelphia, Pennsylvania. Other major exhibitions have been held at the Pace Gallery in New York, the Stedelijk Museum in Amsterdam, and the Whitney Museum of American Art in New York. She has written about life and art in a book called *Writings*, which includes her poetry and thoughts.

Considered to be the father of abstract art, Vassily Kandinsky was what might be considered as a "late bloomer." Born to a family of musicians, he learned to play the piano and cello. As we know, music played an important role in his art. When he was 20 years old he chose to study law and economics and attended the University of Moscow where he lectured and also wrote extensively on spirituality, a subject that also influenced his work. Finally, at the age of 30, Kandinsky left Moscow and went to Munich to study life-drawing, sketching and anatomy. At the age of 37 he had his first exhibition. The artist's unrelenting quest for new forms fueled his passion for painting almost until his death in 1944, at the age of 78.

Henri Rousseau, born in 1844, was a self-taught Sunday painter who began intensive painting when he was 40 years old. He worked as a customs collector where he collected customs fees at a toll station, a job that gave him enough time to paint. Rousseau took the chance to retire at the age of 49 on a small pension to realize his dream of becoming a full-time artist. He tried to supplement his pension by giving violin and painting lessons and by making portraits on commission. He earned some extra money as a street musician. Finally, shortly before Henri's death, the art dealer Ambroise Vollard, with his unerring sense for successful art, bought several of Rousseau's paintings.

A career barraged with many interruptions over a long time can lead to rejection and devastation. The story of Canadian artist Emily Carr who painted expressionist landscapes shows us that aspirations can be ignited anytime. Although Carr felt the urge to paint from an early age her artistic development was halted by ill health and the need to undertake other work to earn a living. Discouraged by years of neglect she had almost ceased to paint. She was captivated when she first saw the work of the Group of Seven, in Toronto at the age of 56. From then on, she worked with renewed energy and deepened spirituality. Today, Emily Carr is highly regarded throughout the world and considered a National Heroine in Canada. She also wrote several autobiographical books.

If wrinkles must be written upon our brows,
let them not be written upon the heart.
The spirit should never grow old.
James A. Garfield

FOUNDATIONS THAT REWARD YEARS OF EFFORT

Several foundations exist to reward mature effort and productivity. The Adolph and Esther Gottlieb Foundation encourages artists who have dedicated their lives to developing their art, regardless of their level of commercial success. It offers two grants for mature painters, printmakers and sculptors. Its Individual Support Grant is for applicants that are able to demonstrate they have been working in a mature phase of their art for at least 20 years. This program was conceived in order to recognize and support the serious, fully-committed artist. The annual deadline for completed application materials is December 15.

The Gottlieb Foundation's Emergency Assistance Program is intended to provide interim financial assistance to qualified artists whose needs are the result of an unforeseen, catastrophic incident, and who lack the resources to meet that situation. Each grant is given as one-time assistance for a specific emergency, examples of which are fire, flood, or emergency medical need. To be eligible for this program, an artist must be able to demonstrate a minimum involvement of 10 years in a mature phase of his or her work. There are no geographical restrictions. It is open to U.S. residents and international artists.

Adolph Gottlieb is regarded as one of the leading Abstract Expressionists. He was a founding member of "New York Artist Painters," a group of abstract painters, including Mark Rothko, and John Graham. He was also a fiercely dedicated artist. At the age of 67, Gottlieb suffered a stroke and was confined to wheelchair with his left side paralyzed, however, he continued painting until his death in 1974.

The Adolph Gottlieb Foundation is located at 380 West Broadway, New York, NY, 10012. Telephone: 212-226-0581. Web site: www.gottliebfoundation.org.

We turn not older with years, but newer every day.
Emily Dickinson

The Pollock-Krasner Foundation was started by the late Lee Krasner, one of the leading abstract expressionist painters and wife of Jackson Pollock in order to aid, internationally, those individuals who have worked as professional artists over a significant period of time. The criteria for the grants are recognizable artistic merit and demonstrable financial need, whether professional, personal or both. There are no deadlines. Throughout the year the Foundation accepts applications from painters, sculptors and artists who work on paper, including printmakers.

The application process includes a cover letter, a completed application, and slides of the artist's most current work.

To obtain application forms and information on the application procedure visit www.pkf.org or write, fax or e-mail your complete mailing address to: The Pollock-Krasner Foundation, Inc., 863 Park Ave., New York, NY 10021. Attn: Request for Application. Fax: 212-288-2836. E-mail: grants@pkf.org.

> *The highest reward for one's toil is not what one gets for it*
> *but what one becomes by it.*
> John Ruskin

The Flintridge Foundation established the Awards for Visual Artists in 1997 to support California, Oregon, and Washington artists of the highest merit. The 2003/2004 recipients range in age from 50 to 73 years. The Foundation distributes ten biennial grants of $25,000 each. Its mission declares, "This program grew from the Foundation's strong belief in the profound dignity and value of a life dedicated to creating a meaningful body of work. The primary goal of the Awards program has been to recognize and support artists and the process of artmaking both directly and indirectly by providing artists with more time and resources to work. These Awards are an acknowledgement not only of extraordinary talent, creativity, and imagination, but also of unflagging courage, optimism, and commitment."

The Flintridge Foundation is located at 1040 Lincoln Avenue, Suite 100, Pasadena, CA 91103. Telephone: 626-449-0839. Fax: 626-585-0011. Awards for Visual Artists (Toll-free): 800-303-2139. www.FlintridgeFoundation.org

More information about grants is available from The Foundation Center www.fdncenter.org and New York Foundation for the Arts www.nyfa.org. *(See Appendix II.)*

Anyone who stops learning is old,
whether at twenty or eighty.
Henry Ford

ADVICE FROM MARGARET DANIELAK, OWNER OF DANIELAKART

Margaret Danielak is the owner of DanielakArt, a personalized art sales and consulting company located in Pasadena, California. She is an Industry Partner member of the American Society of Interior Designers (ASID) and holds a degree in history from the University of California at Berkeley. Her web site is www.danielakart.com.

Her father, the late Robert G. Stevens, worked as a scientific illustrator while he painted the California landscape in his spare time. In 1984 he retired and moved with his wife to Santa Fe, New Mexico where he continued to paint full time. His work is in many collections in Southern California.

After a successful experience selling her father's work, several artists contacted her including the award-winning figurative painter, John Paul Thornton. She was inspired to start DanielakArt, A Gallery Without Walls. "After numerous sales," she stated, "I started a personalized art sales and consulting business in Pasadena, California. I do not own a traditional gallery. Pieces are sold to collectors via exhibitions in alternative venues, at special events, and by personal appointment." Based on her own successful experience in selling the work of mature artists Danielak offers this sage advice:

- **Be proud of your age.** Think positively about your wealth of experience. This experience is what sets you apart from younger artists and can become a large part of what makes you and your work more interesting to potential clients.

- **Make your maturity work for you.** When I sent out press packets for a local show featuring my father's acrylics of the city of Pasadena, I mentioned the fact that he started his art career during World War II by sketching girls from memory for lonely soldiers. I also emphasized that he had been painting for 50 years – information that contributed to the show receiving excellent press coverage.

- **Go out of your way to be friendly.** Wear something that indicates that you are more interesting to talk to than the average person. Dianne Boate, the international designer / photographer I represent, always wears a unique hat of her own design to social events. Every time she does this, people gravitate toward her.

If you feel that galleries reject you in favor of younger artists, Danielak encourages artists to seek out art buyers on their own. She says, "As an artist you will have a great advantage with people who avoid traditional galleries and who prefer to buy their art directly from artists."

Keep on raging to stop the aging. Dale Carnegie

QUICK TIPS ON STAYING YOUNG

- Become a wise sage and you will reduce your age. Share your wisdom, experience and education with younger artists.
- Look for ways to learn from younger artists.
- Keep your mind active by learning new computer programs, reading new periodicals, and attending conferences.
- Keep yourself physically fit and nutritionally healthy. What matters is not how old you are but how young you feel.

CHAPTER 14

THE ART OF COMMUNICATION

My method is to take the utmost trouble
to find the right thing to say,
and then to say it with the utmost levity.
George Bernard Shaw

To succeed as an artist professional communication skills will reward you with harmonious relationships. They include honest discussion, mutual respect and the desire to attain satisfaction on an equal basis. You will want to:

- Be empathetic to the other person's needs and feelings.
- Learn the art of clarification through repetition and ask others to do the same.
- Think before you speak and speak clearly.
- Discuss your needs and expectations with others.
- Feel free to discuss concerns and differences of opinion.
- Aim to resolve conflicting points of view.
- Refrain from hostile or confrontational discussion.
- Ask for what you want by being direct yet cordial.
- Focus on obtaining positive results for all concerned.

Professional courtesy and acts of appreciation are vital, yet often neglected. They include small gestures such as saying "thank you" to guests for attending your exhibition, writers who write your work in an article (no matter how lengthy it is), and colleagues who recommend your work for a commission or sale. Learn to say "thank you" in several foreign languages. They will take you very far in this multi-cultural world.

Telephone communication is an important aspect of doing business. Today, having a message service is a necessity. Make sure your outgoing message sounds clear and professional and allows sufficient time for the caller to leave a message. When you make business calls be prepared with a list of questions and topics. Get into the right frame of mind and focus. Introduce yourself and state the purpose of your call. Be considerate of the person's time – especially writers on deadlines and art dealers preparing for an exhibition opening. Avoid calling too early, too late and during lunchtime. Stand up while speaking if you want to increase your energy level. Smile while you are speaking and relax your jaw. Modulate your speaking tone to avoid a monotone. Speak clearly and succinctly.

Written documents are also essential such as business letters, exhibition and grant proposals, artist's statements, résumés, biographies, promotional brochures, contracts and press releases. Detailed, step-by-step guidelines and many samples of each are in the book *Presentation Power Tools For Fine Artists*. (There is an order form in this book.)

In addition to written and verbal communication much of your communication is *non*-verbal. You communicate through your body posture, movement, facial expression, and personal hygiene. Make direct eye contact and use a firm handshake. Become an attentive listener and express interest in what others are saying. And, always dress in neat, clean and appropriate attire.

An artist cannot speak about his art any more than
a plant can discuss horticulture.

Jean Cocteau

HOW TO DISCUSS YOUR WORK

Robert Henri said: "Your style is the way you talk in paint." The more popular you become the more interested the art community and the art viewing public will be in hearing you talk – in your work and about your work.

You will have many opportunities to discuss your work whether you are involved in social small talk at a gallery opening or in an interview by the press. Your goal is for listeners to take you seriously. This requires preparation. Express your artistic vision with clarity, brevity and poise.

Your "elevator speech" is a brief description of your work in 20 words of less. When Roslyn Rose is asked to describe one of her series of assemblages she says, "I was inspired to honor the histories and myths about women." Regina Noakes says, "My large figurative paintings have references to myself and my daughter." Both descriptions say enough to elicit curiosity and intrigue. You might say the "elevator speech" is the appetizer.

When in-depth information is asked for explain the ideas, content and motivation behind your work using words that create picture images. For example, when Joan Giordano was asked to describe a series of paintings she said, "These pieces emerge from singular cumulative experiences – the vast expanse of ocean, brilliant moss-green fungus, peeling tree bark, skins, crumbling walls and decay. My journey takes me deep into the earth to some ancient place within myself."

ADVICE ON E-MAIL COMMUNICATION

E-mail correspondence offers convenience and immediacy in addition to reducing costs for postage, letterhead and envelopes. Today, we are able to communicate with thousands of individuals around the world with record-breaking speed. However, easy access and speed are no excuses for ignoring many of the professional rules that apply to writing a conventional business letter. Here are some rules that apply to e-mail etiquette:

- Obtain the name, correct spelling and gender of the person you are e-mailing.
- Double check for clarity, accuracy, spelling and grammar.
- Fill out the "subject" heading. Think of it as an important headline in a story. It should catch attention and arouse immediate interest. Avoid using spam "subject" headings.
- Keep your letters concise and to the point. The average person's attention span for reading e-mail is very limited.
- Hyperlinks often go unnoticed. Sending an e-mail with a link to your web site may be very productive to those who know you, however, sending it this way unsolicited is frequently ignored. Instead, introduce yourself and your work by mailing printed visuals with a reference to your web site.
- Get permission first before sending unsolicited attachments with your e-mail. Many people are wary of computer viruses and may ignore your file if they don't know you.
- No one likes spam. If you are sending the same e-mail to several people, hide the other e-mail addresses. Either send them as blind copies or send them individually.
- Don't send e-mail to businesses during the weekend. Your e-mail will get lost in Monday's pile of e-mails.
- Be courteous. Respond to e-mail within 48 hours. If you cannot respond then, send an e-mail to thank them for

their e-mail and say you will respond on or before a specific date. Your provider may offer a service that automatically sends out a response. This is especially useful if you go on vacation and have better things to do than answer e-mail.

That which we are capable of feeling,
we are capable of saying.
Miguel de Cervantes

THE POWER OF KEEPING A JOURNAL

A journal is a powerful tool that enhances your communication skills. A journal affirms the reality of your life. Writing about your life adds meaning. As you write a few thoughts each day your mission and your goals will become crystal clear.

Journaling has the power to quiet the mind and focus your thoughts. It provides ventilation for the annoying chatter that muddles the mind. Writing about your creative conflicts will help you move through them. Writing about your pain will help you to heal. Over time, your journal will reveal the reoccurring obstacles and areas of stress in your life. As you start to notice destructive patterns you can begin to deal with them and ultimately they will lose their control.

The tools you gain from keeping a journal will help you to solve the issues that surface in the process of making your art. The challenges of shaping, balancing, composing, structuring, releasing, beginning and completing will flow more freely. If you have difficulty writing about your work your journal may very well serve as the seeds from which your artist's statement will blossom.

Selected Pages From The Author's Journal

The Healing Power of Art and
My Heartfelt Appreciation to Artists 1999-2005

1999

Art heals. I don't think I've ever before known the true meaning of the words until recently. Art has reached out to me, embraced me, and wrapped itself around me in a cloak of great comfort and consolation.

During the past few years death and mortality have stared at me defiantly and relentlessly. My sister had a mastectomy. I waited in a hospital for six long hours during her surgery. I watched her endure chemotherapy and radiation treatments. After her ordeal, they discovered more "spots" and recommended more surgery and chemo. When I think about those spots, they appear in my mind like huge, black dots racing toward me from a Roy Lichtenstein painting. The thought of her fear and suffering constricts my heart and nearly paralyzes me... Selene eventually lost the battle against Cancer and her two young sons were left to grow up without one of the best mothers that ever lived.

At the same time, I am gradually losing my mother. Physically healthy for her age, her mind is deteriorating from Alzheimer's Disease. She has regressed to the state of a child, unable to fully communicate her emotional and physical feelings.

She doesn't recognize me and doesn't respond to her name, yet she can play several notes to a song on the piano that she hasn't played in fifty years. When I play a cassette of Big Band Sounds she claps her hands. The magic of music is a lifeline to my mother's soul and one of her few joys.

During a disturbing visit with my mother when the energy is tangled by confusion I seek comfort in glancing at a beautiful unsigned abstract sculpture that evokes the human form. Its fluid lines provide a temporary distraction. The shapes undulate against the cool light reflected from the window. What seems like eternity, I become one with the art, escaping into the solid forms and the negative spaces that surround them. My eyes and heart are soothed by the images and their healing qualities.

2000

I recall countless instances at the computer when my gaze drifts above the screen and focuses on a Japanese triptych – a woodblock print by Toyakuni, a student of Hiroshige. Its mystery unfolds before me and helps me to envision a new perspective. Suddenly, the blank computer screen fills up with words. The images before me of the ceremonious Japanese women, gently wrapped in their kimonos, seem to whisper in a form of haiku chant: "Be still, relax, a fountain of words will flow towards you." This piece has carried me through many writing deadlines.

Much of my time is spent on the phone speaking to artists from around the world. I often reflect on a brightly colored photomontage by Anthony Whelihan. The purples, yellows, reds and greens complement each other and create both tension and harmony. Its translucent forms overlap, merge and shift in constant flux that inspires me to be flexible and keep an open mind.

Sensing the experiences and feelings of an artist through their work enhances my life and restores me. Art represents a part of history and expresses the endurance of humanity. I am blessed by knowing artists from around the world who share their gifts with me. I am deeply grateful to artists for their loving devotion to the creative process and their power to heal.

2003

It has been several months since my mother has been able to speak coherently. She often stares into oblivion. Today, aching to find a way to communicate with her, I decided we would do a drawing together. A myriad of memories rushed forth, at the age of four sitting at the kitchen table as she gave me my first finger painting lesson... the paint oozing through my fingers... the magic of colors swirling together on smooth white paper...

Today, I was the teacher and my mother was the student. I picked up a red crayon and drew a heart and colored it. With some coaxing and direction she took a red crayon and drew a heart and colored it. She made three hearts – I'm sure to represent her three children. I said to her, "The heart means love. I love you, Mom. You will always be in my heart." I've told her "I love you" countless times, and she didn't respond, but today the act of drawing the hearts together made a connection. Her eyes welled up with tears as she reached out and took my hand and said, "I love you, too." My heart swelled as tears streamed down my face. Time stopped, and I embraced the poignant, bittersweet, healing moments of bonding with my mother.

When words fail, hearts and souls can be united by making marks on a piece of paper.

November 8, 2005

At 12:35 A.M. my mother surrendered peacefully and painlessly to the sounds of New Age music playing on the CD player, the scent of lavender on her pillow, and poetry and paintings surrounding her. As her breathing gently subsided I stroked her hair, kissed her forehead, and said, "I love you." My heart beat strongly as I imagined hers leaping inside it before she made her journey. I will dedicate many books to her...

APPENDIX I
80 AFFIRMATIONS FOR SUCCESS

I will...
1. Define success in my own terms.
2. Rejoice that I am an artist.
3. Celebrate my unique vision.
4. Nurture my creativity.
5. Strive to reach my potential.
6. View rejection as the opportunity to learn.
7. Ignore destructive criticism.
8. Tame "The Creative Beast."
9. Avoid toxic materials and toxic relationships.
10. Take responsibility for my career.
11. Strive to achieve self-sufficiency.
12. Establish my priorities and put them to memory.
13. Balance my passion, values and life's mission.
14. Create powerful, polished, presentation materials.
15. Take one positive step every day to advance my career.
16. Seize the opportunity to learn from every misfortune.
17. Build strong relationships in the art community.
18. Have the courage to set and accomplish high goals.
19. Set three sets of goals: creative; career; and financial.
20. Create a business plan and keep accurate business records.
21. Increase my knowledge about the business of art.
22. Talk about my art with clarity and enthusiasm.
23. Exude confidence about my work.
24. Follow my vision and build a strong body of work.
25. Continue to grow and groom my mailing list.
26. Contribute time and effort to improve the status of artists.
27. Make my work visible on an on-going basis.
28. Exercise diversity in creating and exhibiting my work.
29. Circulate visual "handouts" of my work continuously.
30. Devise marketing plans with monthly, weekly, and daily activities.
31. Share the benefits of my art to prospective buyers.
32. Contact at least two people each day for business growth.
33. Follow up.
34. Update my résumé and other important documents.
35. Learn the art of polite, yet assertive, self-promotion.
36. Copyright my work.
37. Investigate galleries' reputations before beginning a relationship.
38. Protect my integrity and my art.

39. Share my art with a spirit of generosity.
40. Not wait for art to sell itself.
41. Enhance my networking skills.
42. Stop procrastinating *now!*
43. Reject the myth "the poor starving artist."
44. Reject the myth "I'm an artist, not a business person."
45. Reject the myth "Someday my prince(ss) will come."
46. Develop a healthy partnership with money.
47. Get a grip on my cash flow.
48. Make use of "green power."
49. Exchange support with a network of artists.
50. Share my contacts and information freely with others.
51. Take time to celebrate my accomplishments.
52. Always be prepared for success.
53. Avoid feeling subservient to dealers.
54. Use written consignment agreements.
55. Use proper written contracts.
56. Submit the best quality slides to juried competitions and galleries.
57. Never lie on my résumé.
58. Use my résumé as a sales tool and keep it growing.
59. Avoid over-pricing my work.
60. Refuse to under-value my work.
61. Never sell my work at bargain prices from my studio.
62. Become a successful *Artrepreneur.*
63. Practice the "Rule of Thirds."
64. Become an active artist and art advocate.
65. Raise the volume on self-promotion.
66. Express appreciation to those who help me.
67. Get help from human and technological resources.
68. Sell to and, buy from, fellow artists.
69. View professional success as a journey, not a destination.
70. Make a commitment to my art and my career.
71. Share my vision with collectors and fellow artists.
72. Be a good listener; avoid the need to hear myself speak.
73. Be aware of art events and art news.
74. Be receptive to change.
75. Not burn any bridges.
76. Never give up – ever!
77. Seek the assistance of coaches and the teachings of mentors.
78. Be flexible. When one plan fails, try another.
79. Not rely on one source of power.
80. Not wait to be discovered. I will make it happen!

APPENDIX II RESOURCES

NON-PROFIT ORGANIZATIONS:
ADVOCACY AND LEGAL

ALLIANCE FOR THE ARTS, 330 West 42 St., Suite 1701, New York, NY 10036. Tel: 212-947-6340. Fax: 212-947-6416. www.allianceforarts. org. Dedicated to policy research, information services and advocacy for the arts in NY. Influences the policies and actions of government, funders, and the business of art.

ARTISTS RIGHTS SOCIETY, 536 Broadway, 5th Floor, New York, NY 10012. Tel: 212-420-9160. www.arsny.com. ARS is the preeminent copyright, licensing, and monitoring organization for visual artists in the U.S.

GUERRILLA GIRLS, 532 LaGuardia Pl., #237 New York, NY 10012. www.guerrillagirls.com. Exposes sexism and racism in politics, the art world, film and culture.

NATIONAL ARTISTS EQUITY ASSOCIATION, INC.,PO Box 28068, Central Station, Washington, DC 20005. www.artists-equity.org Advocacy organization for visual artists, with branches throughout the U.S.

NEW YORK ARTISTS EQUITY ASSOCIATION, 498 Broome St., New York, NY 10013. Tel: 212- 941-0130. www.anny.org. Disseminates information regarding legislation and legal rights, all in the interest of effectively addressing "survival" issues relevant to artists. Monitors local, state and federal legislation and strongly advocates bills in support of art and artists.

NEW YORK CITY DEPARTMENT OF CULTURAL AFFAIRS, 330 West 42 St., 14th floor, New York, NY 10036. Tel: 212-643-7770. www.nyc.gov/html/dcla/home.html. Its goals are to sustain and promote the cultural life of the City of New York, and to articulate the contribution made by the cultural community to the City's economic vitality.

U.S. COPYRIGHT OFFICE, Register of copyrights. The Library of Congress, 101 Independence Ave. S.E., Washington, D.C. 20559-6000. 202-707-3000. For copyright forms: 202-707-9100. For information pertaining to copyright law: 202-707-3000. For a basic education in copyright: www.loc.gov/ copyright/

VOLUNTEER LAWYERS FOR THE ARTS, 1 East 53 St., New York, NY 10022. Tel: 212- 319-2787. www. vlany.org. Offers assistance to low-income artists. Art Law Line provides quick answers to legal questions.

NON-PROFIT ORGANIZATIONS:
WITH FUNDING AND OTHER SUPPORT SERVICES

THE AMERICAN ACADEMY IN ROME, 7 East 60 St., New York, NY 10022. Tel: 212- 751-7200. www. aarome.org. The only American overseas center for independent study and advanced research in the fine arts and the humanities.

ART IN EMBASSIES PROGRAM, Department of State, OBO/OM/ART, Washingon, D.C. 20522-0611 Tel:703-875-4202. Lends art to embassies worldwide.

THE ARTISTS COMMUNITY FEDERAL CREDIT UNION, 351 A West 54 St., 1st floor, New York, NY 10019. Tel: 212-246-3344. Federally insured credit union that assists artists in establishing a credit rating.

ARTS & BUSINESS COUNCIL, 520 Eighth Ave., Suite 319, New York, NY 10018. T: 212-279-5910 www.artsandbusiness.org. Stimulates partnerships between the arts and business that strengthen both sectors in the communities they serve.

THE BUSINESS COMMITTEE FOR THE ARTS, INC. (BCA), 29-27 Queens Plaza North, 4th Floor, LIC, N Y 11101. Tel: 718-482-9900. Fax: 718-482-9911. www.bcainc.org. Fosters business/arts alliances through research, publications, seminars and conferences. Guides companies in their investments in the arts.

BRONX COUNCIL ON THE ARTS, 1738 Hone Ave., Bronx, NY 10461. Tel: 718-931-9500. www.bronxarts. org. The officially designated arts council of the Bronx. Provides exhibitions and business workshops for artists.

CITYARTS, INC. 525 Broadway, Suite 700 New York, NY 10012. Tel: 212-966-0377. www.cityarts.org. Creates public art of the highest caliber in communities where access to and participation in the arts are limited.

FLINTRIDGE FOUNDATION, 1040 Lincoln Avenue, Suite 100, Pasadena, CA 91103. Tel: 626-449-0839. Fax: 626-585-0011. www.flintridge foundation.org. Awards for Visual Artists (Toll-free): 800-303-2139. The Foundation distributes ten biennial grants of $25,000 each to support California, Oregon, and Washington artists of the highest merit.

FLUSHING COUNCIL ON CULTURE & THE ARTS, 137-35 Northern Blvd., Flushing, NY 11354. Tel: 718-463-7700. www.flushing townhall.org. Makes the arts a central part of life for developing the arts in the community. Presents exhibitions, seminars and offers technical assistance to artists.

THE FOUNDATION CENTER, 79 Fifth Ave., 2nd floor, New York, NY 10003. Tel: 212-620-4230. www.fdncenter.org. Resource center for information about funding opportunities.

ADOLPH AND ESTHER GOTTLIEB FOUNDATION, 380 W. Broadway, New York, NY 10012. Tel: 212-226-0581. Provides financial support to individual artists who have shown a lifetime of commitment to their art.

THE ELIZABETH GREENSHIELDS FOUNDATION, 1814 Sherbrooke West, Ste. 1, Montreal, Quebec, Canada H3H 1E4. Tel: 514-937-9225. Fax: 514-937-0141. E: egreen@total.net. Promotes, by charitable activities carried on by the Foundation, an appreciation of the traditional expression in painting, drawing, sculpture and the graphic arts, by aiding worthy art students, artists or sculptors who need further training or other assistance during their formative years.

JOHN SIMON GUGGENHEIM MEMORIAL FOUNDATION, Art Department, Scholarship/Grant Program, 90 Park Ave., New York, NY 10016. Tel: 212- 687-4470. www.gf. org. Offers fellowships to further the development of scholars and artists.

MATERIALS FOR THE ARTS, 33-00 Northern Blvd., 3rd floor, Long Island City, N.Y. 11101. Tel: 718-729-3001. Fax: 718-729-3941. www.mfta.org. Provides over 2,700 arts programs with the things they need to prosper and endure. Gathers materials from companies that no longer need them, and distributes them to artists and educators.

NATIONAL ENDOWMENT FOR THE ARTS Exists to foster, preserve, and promote excellence in the arts, to bring art to all Americans, and to provide leadership in arts education. The nation's largest annual funder of the arts, bringing art to all 50 states, including rural areas, inner cities, and military bases.

NEW YORK FOUNDATION FOR THE ARTS, 155 Ave. of the Americas, New York, NY 10013. Tel: 212-366-6900. www.nyfa.org. Fellowships, residencies, project support, loans, fiscal sponsorship of small to medium sized arts organizations, and information services for artists and organizations in all artistic areas in the U.S.

NEW YORK STATE COUNCIL ON THE ARTS (NYSCA), 175 Varick St. New York, NY 10014.Tel: 212-627-4455. Promotes and develops New York's cultural, economic and human resources through support of the arts. Funds non-profit organizations to provide cultural services, and awards grants in the performing and visual arts.

POLLOCK-KRASNER FOUNDATION, 863 Park Ave., New York, NY 10021. Tel: 212-517-5400. www.pkf.org. Provides financial assistance to individual working artists of established ability through the generosity of the late Lee Krasner, one of the leading abstract expressionist painters and widow of Jackson Pollock.

THE PUBLIC ART FUND, 1 East 53 St., 11th floor, NY, NY 10022. Tel: 212- 980-4575. www.publicartfund. org. Promotes the use of art in public spaces in New York City.

QUEENS COUNCIL ON THE ARTS Oak Ridge at Forest Park, One Forest Park, Woodhaven, NY 11421. Tel: 718-647-3377. www.queens councilarts.org. Supports, promotes, and develops the arts in Queens County. Assists arts organizations and individual artists and presents its diverse cultural resources.

THE MARIE WALSH SHARPE ART FOUNDATION 830 North Tejon Street, Suite 120, Colorado Springs, CO 80903. Tel: 719-635-3220 www.sharpeartfdn.org. Offers free studio spaces in Manhattan.

VISUAL AIDS, 526 West 26 St., #510, New York, NY 10001. Tel: 212-627-9855. Fax: 212-627-9815. www.visualaids.org. Strives to increase public awareness of AIDS through the visual arts, creating programs of exhibitions, events and publications, and working in partnership with artists, galleries, museums and AIDS organizations.

THE WORLD STUDIO FOUNDATION, 200 Varick St., #507, New York, NY 10014. Tel: 212-366-1317. www.worldstudio.org. Gives scholarships to minority and economically disadvantaged students.

Non-Profit Organizations
With Membership Services

ALLIANCE OF QUEENS ARTISTS (AQA), 99-10 Metropolitan Ave., Forest Hills, NY 11375. Tel: 718-520-9842. Fax: 718-261-6166. www.arts4u.org. Dedicated to the creation and promotion of the visual arts. Presents exhibitions and other events.

AMERICAN ARTISTS PROFESSIONAL LEAGUE, (AAPL), C/O Salmagundi Club, 47 Fifth Ave., New York, NY 10003. Tel: 212-645-1345. The country's authority on artist's pigments. Sets the standards for pigments and artists materials.

AMERICAN CRAFT COUNCIL, 72 Spring, St., 6th floor, New York, NY 10012. Tel: 212-274-0630. Conducts juried exhibitions, offers group rates on insurance, co-publishes *The Voice* and operates a slide registry on American craft artists.

THE AMERICAN FEDERATION OF ARTS (AFA), 41 East 65 St., New York, NY 10021. Tel: 212-988-7700. www.afaweb.org. The nation's oldest and most comprehensive museum service organization.

AMERICAN INSTITUTE OF GRAPHIC ARTS, 164 Fifth Ave., New York, NY 10010. Tel: 212-807-1990. www.aiga.org. Promotes graphic design in books and other media, with many chapters throughout the U.S.

AMERICAN INSTITUTE OF ARCHITECTS (AIA), New York Chapter, 536 La Guardia Place, New York, NY 10012. Tel: 212- 683-0023. www.aiany.org. Provides a wide range of educational programs for members and the general public.

AMERICAN SOCIETY OF CONTEMPORARY ARTISTS, (ASCA), C/O V. Lubrano, President, 130 Gale Pl., 9-H, Bronx, NY 10463. Tel: 718-548-6790. www.anny.org/asca/artist. Exhibits the varied currents of 20th century art in galleries and alternative spaces.

AMERICAN WATERCOLOR SOCIETY, C/O Salmagundi Club, 47 Fifth Ave., NY, NY 10003. Tel: 212- 206-8986. Oldest and largest watercolor society. Advances watercolor painting, awards scholarships, holds demonstrations and a national watercolor exhibition.

ART DEALERS ASSOCIATION OF AMERICA (ADAA), 575 Madison Ave., New York, NY 10022. Tel: 212-940-8590. www.artdealers.org. A membership organization of the nation's leading galleries in the fine arts. Seeks to promote the highest standards of connoisseurship, scholarship and ethical practice within the profession.

THE ART INFORMATION CENTER, Director Dan Concholar, 55 Mercer St., 3rd floor, New York, NY 10013. Tel: 212- 966-3443. Advises artists on New York galleries.

ARTISTS SPACE, 38 Greene St., 3rd floor, New York, NY 10013. Tel: 212-226-3970. www.artistsspace.org Non-profit organization with a gallery and computerized Artists File.

ARTISTS TALK ON ART, (ATOA), 10 Waterside Plaza, #33D, New York, NY 10010. Tel: 212- 779-9250. Presents panel discussions comprised of leading art professionals on current and vital art issues.

ART TABLE, INC., 270 Lafayette St., Suite 608, New York, NY 10012. Tel: 212-343-1735. Fax: 212-343-1430. www.arttable.org. A national organization for professional women in the visual arts. Membership is available by invitation only.

ASSOCIATION OF HISPANIC ARTS, INC. 220 East 106 St., 3rd floor, New York, NY 10029. Tel: 212-876-1242. F: 212-876-1285. www.latinoarts.org. Advances Latino arts, artists and art organizations as an integral part of the cultural life of the nation. Facilitates projects and programs designed to foster the appreciation, growth and well being of the Latino cultural community.

BROOKLYN WORKING ARTISTS COALITION (BWAC), PO Box 020072, Brooklyn, NY 11202. Tel: 718-596-2507. www.bwac.org. Supports the growth of the visual arts by sponsoring exhibitions and educational programs. Provides a conduit between working Brooklyn artists and the community at large.

BURR ARTISTS, C/O Fred Schwartz, President, 325 West 86th St., #12B, New York, NY 10024. Tel: 212-877-3527. Exhibits members' work of varied styles and media in exhibitions throughout NYC.

CHICAGO ARTISTS' COALITION, 11 East Hubbard St., 7th floor, Chicago, IL 60611. Tel: 312-670-2060. Artist-run coalition of visual artists and friends. It provides educational, advocacy and professional services. Publishes *The Chicago Artists' News,* a monthly newsletter, and several resource books for artists.

COLLEGE ART ASSOCIATION OF AMERICA, 275 Seventh Ave., New York, NY 10001.Tel: 212-691-1051. E: newyorkoffice@collegeart.org www.collegeart.org. Promotes and enhances excellence in the practice and teaching aspects of art and art history. Publishes *Art Bulletin, Artjournal* and *CAA Careers.*

CREATIVE TIME, 307 Seventh Ave., #1904, New York, NY 10001. Tel: 212-206-6674. www.creative time.org. Presents writers, visual artists, architects, and performing artists in unusual collaborations.

CRYSTAL QUILT, 532 LaGuardia Place, #321, New York, NY 10012. Tel: 212-941-4994. www.crystal quilt.org. A feminist organization that designs educational and cultural programs that speak to women's desires for meaning, connection and power. Presents a wide range of discussions, workshops and support

groups, literary readings, performances and other cultural events.

EN FOCO, 32 East Kingsbridge Rd., Bronx, New York 10468. Tel/Fax: 718-584-7718. www.enfoco.org. A non-profit photography organization whose commitment to photography brings you outstanding work by photographers of African, Asian, Latino and Native American heritage.

GEN ART, Art of The Next Generation, 133 West 25 St., New York, NY 10001.Tel: 212- 255-7300. www.gen art.org. Promotes young emerging artists, filmmakers and fashion designers.

GRAPHIC ARTISTS GUILD, 90 John St., Suite 403, New York, NY 10038. Tel: 212-791-3400. www. gag.org. Improves conditions for all creators of graphic art, and raises standards for the entire industry.

INTERNATIONAL FINE PRINT DEALERS ASSOCIATION (IFPDA), 15 Gramercy Park So., Ste.7A, New York, NY 10003. Tel: 212-674-6095. www.printdealers.com. Ensures the highest ethical standards and quality among fine print dealers, and promotes greater appreciation of fine prints among art collectors and the general public.

INTERNATIONAL SCULPTURE CENTER, 14 Fairgrounds Rd., #B, Hamilton, NJ 08619. Tel: 609-689-1051. www.sculpture.org. Advances the creation and understanding of sculpture.

LOWER MANHATTAN CULTURAL COUNCIL, One Wall Street Ct., second floor, New York, NY 10005. Tel: 212- 219-9401. www.lmcc.net. Public planning, advocacy and source for funding, services, creation and presentation opportunities for artists and small arts groups throughout Manhattan's diverse neighborhoods.

NATIONAL ART LEAGUE, 44-21 Douglaston Parkway, Douglaston, NY 11363. Tel: 718-224-3957. www. nationalartleague.org. An organization for professional artists, serious students and those interested in participating in and supporting the advancement of the creative arts of drawing, painting and sculpture.

NATIONAL ASSOCIATION OF ARTISTS' ORGANIZATIONS, C/O Space One Eleven, 2409 Second Ave, North Birmingham, AL 35203.E: info@naao.net. www.naao.net Membership organization consisting of organizations and artists. Provides information on legislative issues and government policies affecting artists and art organizations.

NATIONAL ASSOCIATION OF WOMEN ARTISTS (NAWA), 80 Fifth Ave., Suite 1405, New York, NY 10011.Tel/Fax: 212-675-1616. www. nawanet.org. The oldest and largest women artists exhibiting organization. Encourages and promotes the creative output of women artists.

NATIONAL SCULPTURE SOCIETY, 237 Park Ave., New York, NY 10017. Tel: 212-764-5645. Fax: 212-764-5651. www.sculpturereview. com/nss.htm. Promotes excellence in figurative and realist sculpture throughout the US. Sponsors exhibitions, publishes *Sculpture Review,* provides academic scholarships, and operates the National Sculpture Society gallery.

THE NATIONAL SOCIETY OF PAINTERS IN CASEIN AND ACRYLIC. Gives artists working in these mediums the opportunity to exhibit works regardless of style, "school", or subject matter. Full membership is by invitation only. For Associate Membership information send a #10 SASE to Robert Sanstrom, 377 West Chester Ave., Port Chester, NY 10573. For a prospec-

tus for the Juried Exhibition send a #10 SASE to Douglas Wiltraut, President NSPCA, 969 Catasauqua Rd., Whitehall, PA 18052.

NEW YORK SOCIETY OF WOMEN ARTISTS, an organization of NYC area professional women artists. Artists who work in 2-d art contact Lynne Friedman, 414 Circle Ave Kingston, NY 12401. Artists who work in 3-d art contact Janet Indick, 428 Sagamore Ave., Teaneck, NJ 07666. E-mail: nyswa @aol.com.

NURTURE ART, 160 Cabrini Blvd. PH 134, New York, NY 10033. Tel: 212-795-5566. www.nurtureart.org. Provides exposure and support for artists.

PASTEL SOCIETY OF AMERICA, C/O National Arts Club, 15 Gramercy Park, New York, NY 10003. Tel: 212- 533-6931. www.pastel societyofamerica.org. Encourages the use of pastel and educates the public regarding the permanence and beauty of pastels.

PEN & BRUSH CLUB, 16 East 10 St., New York, NY 10003. Tel: 212-475-3669. Fax: 212- 475-6018. www.penandbrush.org. The oldest organization of professional women in the arts in the U.S.

PRINTED MATTER, 535 West 22 St., New York, NY 10011. Tel: 212-925-0325. www.printedmatter.org. The world's largest non-profit facility dedicated to the promotion of publications made by artists in a book-like format. Fosters the appreciation, dissemination, and understanding of publications made by artists.

PROFESSIONAL WOMEN PHO-TOGRAPHERS, C/O Photographics Unlimited, 17 West 17 St., NY, NY 10011. www.pwponline.org. Educates, supports, and encourages the work of women photographers of all concentrations.

SALUTE to WOMEN IN THE ARTS, President: Rosemary Zabal: Tel: 201-891-8689. www.salutetowomen inthearts.com. An environment in which male and female artists meet their peers, share ideas and experiences, and make career contacts vital to artistic growth.

SCULPTORS GUILD, SoHo Building, 110 Greene St., #601, 10012. Tel/Fax: 212-431-5669. www.sculptorsguild.org. Promotes and encourages contemporary sculpture by providing a forum and showcase for its members.

SOCIETY OF ILLUSTRATORS, 128 East 63 St., New York, NY 10021. Tel: 212- 838-2560. www.society illustrators.org. An international organization of illustrators, photographers and art directors.

CATHARINE LORILLARD WOLFE ART CLUB, INC., 802 Broadway, New York, NY 10003. www.clwac.org. Women artists' organization with exhibitions.

WOMEN'S CAUCUS FOR ART (WCA) National Chapter, P.O. Box 1498 Canal Street Station, New York, NY 10013. Tel: 212- 634-0007. www.nationalwca.com. Membership organization with chapters nationwide and an emphasis on women working in the visual arts professions today.

WOMEN'S STUDIO CENTER, Entrance: 21-25 44 Ave., Long Island City, NY 11101. Mailing: 43-32 22 St., Long Island City, NY 11101. Tel: 718-361-5649. www.womenstudiocenter.org. Fine arts studio and membership organization that provides information about women in the arts to artists, the art world and the general public. Publishes *Women's Art News.*

RESIDENCIES

THE MILLAY COLONY FOR THE ARTS, INC., 454 East Hill Rd., PO Box 3, Austerlitz, NY 12017. Tel: 518-392-3103. www.millaycolony. org. Gives residencies to visual and performing artists, writers and composers.

VERMONT STUDIO CENTER, PO Box 613, Johnson, VT 05656. Tel: 802-635- 2727. www.vermontstudio center.org. Gives residencies to visual artists and writers.

EDWARD F. ALBEE FOUNDATION, 14 Harrison St., New York, NY 10013. "The Barn" residence for writers, painters, sculptors and composers. For application go to www. pipeline.com/~jtnyc/albeefdtn.html

RECOMMENDED PERIODICALS

Afterimage, 31 Prince St., Rochester, NY 14607. Tel: 716-442-8676. www.vsw.org/afterimage/ Bi-monthly journal of media arts and cultural criticism.

American Artist, 770 Broadway, New York, NY 10036. Tel: (800) 745-8922. Monthly magazine.

American Style, The Rosen Group, 3000 Chestnut Ave., Suite 304, Baltimore, MD 21211. Tel: 410-243-7089. www.americanstyle.com Quarterly magazine.

Aperture, 20 East 23 St., New York, NY 10010. Tel: 212- 505-5555. Quarterly photography publication.

Art and Auction, 11 East 36 St., 9th floor, New York, NY 10016.Tel: 212-447-9555. Monthly magazine.

Art Business News, 60 Ridgeway Plaza, Stamford, CT 06905. Tel: 213-356-1745. Monthly magazine.

Art Calendar: *The Business Magazine for Visual Artists*, PO Box 2675, Salisbury, MD 21802. www.art calendar.com. Monthly magazine.

Art Deadlines List, Resources, Box 381067, Harvard Sq. Station, Cambridge, MA 02238. www.ArtDead linesList.com. A monthly resource list. Available in paper and by e-mail.

Artforum, 350 Seventh Ave. New York, NY 10001. Tel: 212-475-4000. www.artforum.com Monthly magazine.

Art In America, 575 Broadway, New York, NY 10012. Tel: 212-941-2806. Monthly magazine.

Art In America Guide To Museums, Galleries & Artists, published in August by *Art in America*. Tel: 212- 941-2800.

The Artist's Magazine, 1507 Dana Ave., Cincinnati, OH 45207. Monthly magazine.

ARTnews, LIC, 48 West 38 St., New York, NY 10018.Tel: 800-284-4625. www.artnews.com. Monthly magazine.

Art Now Gallery Guide, 97 Grayrock Rd., PO Box 5541, Clinton, NJ 08809. Tel: 908-638-5255. www. galleryguide.org. Monthly guide.

Art Times, CSS Publications, Inc., PO Box 730, Mt. Marion, NY 12456. Tel: 845-246-6944. www.arttimesjournal.com E: info@arttimesjournal.com Monthly newspaper.

Entrepreneur: The Small Business Authority, Tel: 800-274-6229. www.entrepreneurmag.com

F.Y.I., published by the New York Foundation for the Arts, 155 Avenue of the Americas, New York, NY 10013. T: 212-366-6900. W: www.nyfa.org. Bi-monthly newsletter.

Gallery & Studio, *The World of the Working Artist,* published by Eye Level Ltd., 217 East 85, PBM, New York, NY 10028. Bi-monthly magazine. Tel: 212- 861-6814. E: gallery-andstudio@mindspring.com.

Photograph, 64 West 89 St., #3F, New York, NY 10025. Tel: 212-787-0481. www.photography-guide.com Bi-monthly U.S. photography guide.

The Photo Review 140 East Richardson Ave. #301, Langhorne, PA 19047. Tel: 215-891-0214. www.photoreview.org. Monthly newsletter.

Sculpture Magazine, published by International Sculpture Center. Tel: 212-785-1144. Monthly magazine.

Sculpture Review, published by the National Sculpture Society 1177 Avenue of the Americas, New York, NY 10036. Tel: 212-764-5645. Quarterly magazine.

STATISTICS: *Gender Discrimination in the Art Field* by Eleanor Dickinson. It may be ordered from her for $7.00 in the U.S. Write to her at 2125 Broderick St., San Francisco, CA 94115 or e-mail: eleanordickinson @Mac.com.

Sunshine Artist, published by Palm House Publishing, 3210 Dade Ave., Orlando, FL 32804. Tel: 800-804-4607. www.sunshineartist.com Monthly magazine.

Woman's Art Journal, Elsa Honig Fine, Editor and Publisher, 1711 Harris Road, Laverock, PA 19038. www. womansartjournal.org. Published May and November.

Women's Art News, Published by Women's Studio Center, 43-22 22 St., Long Island City, NY 11101. Tel: (718) 361-5649. www.womenstudio center.org. Monthly newsletter.

RECOMMENDED INTERNET RESOURCES

ArtDeadline.com
www.artdeadline.com
Income and exhibition opportunities available in print form or online.

Art Deadlines List
ArtDeadlinesList.com
A monthly newsletter (via e-mail or paper) with 600-900 announcements

Artist Help Network
www.artisthelpnetwork.com
Free information service

Artjobs
www.onelist.com/subscribe.cgi/ ARTJOBS
Free subscription service that posts job opportunities on its website.

ArtLex - Dictionary of Visual Art
www.artlex.com Reference material in art, art history, art criticism, aesthetics and art education.

Artnet Magazine
www.artnet.com
Art world news and articles.

Artswire
www.artswire.org
Communications network for the arts community.

The Foundation Center
www.fdncenter.org
Non-profit clearinghouse for grant and fund-raising information.

Gamblin Colors
www.gamblincolors.com
Information on the techniques used by master artists, studio safety, and conservation science.

Manhattan Arts International
www.ManhattanArts.com
Artists' resources, articles, book excerpts.

World Wide Arts Resources
wwar.com
The largest marketplace for contemporary art, international art news, research and gallery portfolios.

RECOMMENDED BOOKS

303 Marketing Tips: Guaranteed to Boost Your Business by Rieva Lesonsky and Leann Anderson. Published by Entrepreneur.

365 Ways to Simplify Your Work Life by Odette Pollar. Published by Dearborn.

The A-Z of Art: The World's Greatest & Most Popular Artists & Their Works by Nicola Hodge and Libby Anson. Published by Advanced Marketing Services, Inc.

A Guide to Art: A Handy Reference to Artists, Their Works, and Artistic Movements by Sandro Sproccati. Published by Abrams.

American Art Directory. Published by National Register Publishing. www.americanartdir.com

And I Quote compiled by Ashton Appewhite, William R. Evans III, and Andrew Frothingham. Published by St. Martin's Press.

Art and Healing: *Using Expressive Art to Heal Your Body, Mind and Spirit,* by Barbara Ganim. Published by Three Rivers Press.

Art and Its Histories: A Reader by Steve Edwards. Published by Yale University Press.

Art and Photography by Aaron Scharf. Published by Viking Penguin.

Art and Reality: *The New Standard Reference Guide and Business Plan for Actively Developing Your Career as an Artist* by Robert J. Abbott. Published by Seven Lock.

The ArtFair SourceBook: The Definitive Guide to Fine Art & Contemporary Craft Shows in the United States published by Sourcebook Publishing Company.

Art Information and the Internet: *How to Find It, How to Use It* by Lois Swan Jones. Published by Onyx Press.

Artist's and Graphic Designer's Market edited by Mary Cox. Published by F & W.

Artists and Writers Colonies published by Blue Heron Press.

Artists' Bookkeeping Book published by Chicago Artists Coalition. Tel: 312-670-2060. www.caconline. org

Artists' Communities Directory published by The Alliance of Artists' Communities, Portland, Oregon.

The Artist's Complete Health and Safety Guide by Monona Rossol. Published by Allworth Press, 1990.

Artist to Artist: *Inspiration and Advice from Artists Past and Present* compiled by Clint Brown. Published by Jackson Creek Press.

The Artist-Gallery Partnership: *A Practical Guide To Consigning Art,* by Tad Crawford and Susan Mellon. Published by Allworth Press.

The Artist's Friendly Legal Guide by Floyd Conner et al. Published by North Light Books.

Artists' Gallery Guide published by Chicago Artists Coalition. Tel: 312-670-2060. www.caconline.org

The Artist's Guide to New Markets: *Opportunities to Show and Sell Art Beyond Galleries* by Peggy Hadden. Published by Allworth Press.

The Artist's Resource Handbook by Daniel Grant. Published by Allworth Press.

Artists' Self-Help Guide published by Chicago Artists Coalition. Tel: 312-670-2060. www.caconline.org

The Artist's Survival Manual: *A Complete Guide To Marketing Your Work* by Toby Judith Klayman. Published by Charles Scribner's Sons.

The Artist's Way: *A Spiritual Path to Higher Creativity* by Julia Cameron. Published by Tarcher/Pedigree Books.

Art Law: *The Guide for Collectors, Investors, Dealers and Artists,* by Ralph E. Lerner and Judith Bresler. Published by Practicing Law Institute.

Art Marketing Handbook: *Marketing Art in the Nineties* by Calvin J. Goodman and Florence J. Goodman. Published by Gee Tee Be.

Art Marketing 101: *A Handbook For The Fine Artist,* by Constance Smith. Published by Art Network.

Artspeak by Robert Atkins. Published by Abbeyville Press.

Arts Wire Web Manual published by New York Foundation for the Arts. 212- 366-6900.

Art Talk-Conversations with 15 Women Artists by Cindy Nemser. Published by Harper Collins.

The Business of Art edited by Lee Caplin. Published by Prentice-Hall.

Business and Legal Forms For Fine Artists by Tad Crawford. Published by Allworth Press.

Business and Legal Forms For Photographers by Tad Crawford. Published by Allworth Press.

The Business of Being an Artist, by Daniel Grant. Published by Allworth Press.

Career Solutions for Creative People How to Balance Artistic Goals with Career Security, by Dr. Ronda Ormont. Published by Allworth Press.

The Complete Guide To New York Art Galleries by Renée Phillips. Published by Manhattan Arts International. *(See page 231.)*

The Complete Idiot's Guide to Starting Your Own Business by Ed Paulson and Marcia Layton. Published by Macmillan Publishing Co

The Concise Oxford Dictionary of Art and Artists by Ian Chilvers. Published by Oxford University Press, Inc.

The CraftFair SourceBook The Definitive Guide to Traditional and Country Craft Shows in the U.S. Published by Sourcebook Publishing Company.

Crafting as a Business by Wendy Rosen. Published by The Rosen Group, Inc.

The Crafts Business Answer Guide & Resource Guide by Barbara Brabec. Published by M. Evans and Company, Inc.

The Crafts Supply SourceBook: A Comprehensive Shop-by-Mail Guide for Thousands of Craft Materials by Margaret Ann Boyd. Published by F&W.

Chronicles of Courage: Very Special Artists by Jean Kennedy Smith and George Plimpton. Foreword by Robert Coles. Published by Random House.

Creative Cash: How to Profit from Your Special Artistry, Creativity, Hand Skills, and Related Know-How by Barbara Brabec. Published by Prima Publishing.

Everything's Organized by Lisa Kanarek. Published by Career Press, Inc.

Finding Your Perfect Work: The New Career Guide to Making a Living, Creating a Life by Paul Edwards and Sarah Edwards. Published by Putnam Publishing Group.

Fine Art Publicity: The Complete Guide For Galleries And Artists by Susan Abbott and Barbara Webb. Published by the Art Business News.

The Fine Artist's Career Guide by Daniel Grant. Published by Allworth Press.

The Fine Artist's Guide To Marketing And Self-Promotion by Julius Vitali. Published by Allworth Press.

The Fine Artist's Guide To Showing And Selling Your Work by Sally Prince Davis. Published by North Light Books.

From the Center: Feminist Essays on Women's Art by Lucy Lippard. Published by E.P. Dutton, Inc.

Foundry Guide & Directory An A to Z Comparison of 100 Foundries Published by International Sculpture Center.

Get the Message: *A Decade of Art for Social Change* by Lucy R. Lippard. Published by E.P. Dutton, Inc.

Go Wild! Creative Opportunities for Artists in the Out-of-Doors compiled by Bonnie Fournier. Published by Lucky Dog Multi-Media.

Grant-Searching Simplified by S.B. Wolfe. Published by Creative Resources, Clyde, NC.

Herstory: *Women Who Changed The World* by Ruth Ashby and Deborah Gore Ohrn. Introduction by Gloria Steinem. Published by Viking.

How to Get Started Selling Your Art by Carole Katchen. Published by F & W.

How to Handle 1,000 Things at Once: *A Fun Guide to Mastering Home & Personal Management* by Don Aslett. Published by Marsh Cree.

How To Photograph Your Art by Malcolm Lubliner. Published by Pomegranate Press.

How To Photograph Your Artwork by Kim Brown. Published by Canyonwinds.

How To Start and Succeed As An Artist by Daniel Grant. Published by Allworth Press.
How To Survive and Prosper as an Artist by Caroll Michels. Published by Henry Holt and Company.

Inside The Art World: *Conversations With Barbaralee Diamonstein* published by Rizzoli.

Juried Art Exhibitions: Ethical Guidelines & Practical Applications published by Chicago Artists Coalition. Tel: 312-670-2060. www.caconline.org

Legal Guide for the Visual Artist by Tad Crawford. Published By Allworth Press.

Life, Paint and Passion: *Reclaiming The Magic of Spontaneous Expression* by Michell Cassou and Stewart Cubley. Published by G. P. Putnam's Sons.

Lives and Works: Talks with Women Artists Vol. 2 by Joan Arbeiter, Beryl Smith and Sally Shearer Swenson. Published by Scarecrow Press, Inc.

Marketing Made Easier: Guide to Free Organizing Artists published by National Association of Artists' Organizations.

The McGraw-Hill Guide to Starting Your Own Business: *A Step-by-Step Blueprint for the First-Time Entrepreneur* by Stephen C. Harper. Published by McGraw-Hill.

Money For Visual Artists published by Americans for the Arts with Allworth Press.

New York Publicity Outlets published by Public Relations Plus, Inc.

Organizing From The Right Side of The Brain: *A Creative Approach to Getting Organized* by Lee Silber. Published by Thomas Dunne Books.

Overexposure: Health Hazards in Photography by Susan Shaw. Published by Allworth Press.

The Official Museum Directory, published by National Register Publishing. www.officialmuseumdir.com

The Overwhelmed Person's Guide to Time Management by Ronnie Eisenberg. Published by NAL/Dutton.

The Oxford Dictionary of Art edited by Ian Chilvers, Harold Osborne, and Dennis Farr. Published by Oxford University Press.

Photographer's Market: 2,000 Places to Sell Your Photographs edited by Megan Lane. Published by F & W.

Photographing Your Artwork: A Step-By-Step Guide to Taking High Quality Slides at an Affordable Price by Russell Hart. Published by North Light.

The Pink Glass Swan by Laucy R. Lippard. Published by The New Press.

The Positive Principle Today by Norman Vincent Peale. Published by Fawcett Book Group.

The Power of Feminist Art by Norma Broude and Mary D. Gerrard. Published by Harry N. Abrams, Inc.

Presentation Power Tools For Fine Artists: *Step-by-Step Professional Advice & Samples* by Renée Phillips. Published by Manhattan Arts. *(See information on page 230.)*

Professional's Guide To Publicity by Richard Winer. Published by Public Relations Publishing Co.

The Prophet, by Kahlil Gibran. Published by Alfred A. Knopf, Inc.

The Publicity Manual by Kate Kelly. Published by Visibility Enterprises.

The Road Less Traveled, by M. Scott Peck, MD. Published by Simon & Schuster.

The Seven Habits of Highly Effective People by Stephen R. Covey. Published by Simon & Schuster.

The Seven Spiritual Laws of Success: A Practical Guide to the Fulfillment of Your Dreams by Deepak Chopra. Published by Amber-Allen Publishing and New World Library.

Small Business for Dummies by Eric Tyson and Jim Schell. Published by IDG Books Worldwide.

Spirit Taking Form: Making A Spiritual Practice of Making Art by Nancy Azara. Published by Red Wheel.

Taking The Leap: The Insider's Guide To Exhibiting And Selling Your Art, By Cay Lang. Published by Chronicle Books.

The Thames and Hudson Dictionary of Art Terms (World of Art), by Edward Lucie-Smith. Published by Thames & Hudson.

Time Management for Busy People by Roberta Roesch. Published by McGraw-Hill Companies, Inc.

Time Management for The Creative Person by Lee Silber. Published by Three Rivers Press.

Time Management for Dummies by Jeffrey J. Mayer. Published by IDG Books Worldwide.

Ulrich's International Periodicals Directory published by R.R. Bowker.

Unstoppable: 45 Powerful Stories of Perseverance and Triumph from People Just Like You by Cynthia Kersey. Published by Sourcebooks.

A Visual Artists' Guide to Estate Planning, published by the Marie Walsh Sharpe Foundation and the Judith Rothschild Foundation. Tel: 719-635-3220.

Wage Slave No More!: Law and Taxes For The Self-Employed by Stephen Fishman. Published by Nolo Press.

Why Have There Been No Great Women Artists? by Linda Nochlin. Published by Collier.

Women, Art and Society by Whitney Chadwick. Published by Thames & Hudson.

Working Mothers 101: How To Organize Your Life, Your Children, And Your Career To Stop Feeling Guilty And Start Enjoying It All by Katherine Wyse Goldman. Published by Harper Collins.

Working Smart: How to Accomplish More in Half the Time by Michael LeBoeuf. Published by Warner Brooks, Inc.

Working Solo: The Real Guide to Freedom and Financial Success with Your Own Business, by Terri Lonier. Published by John Wiley & Sons.

Young Millionaires: Inspiring Stories To Ignite Your Entrepreneurial Dreams by Rieva Lesonsky and Gayle Sato Stodder. Published by Entrepreneur Media.

The Zen of Creativity: Cultivating Your Artistic Life by John Daido Loori. Published by Ballantine Books.

The Zen of Creative Painting by Jeanne Carbonetti. Published by Watson-Guptil.

PROFESSIONAL SERVICES

PRINTING

Graphic Lab Digital Communications
228 East 45 St., New York, NY 10017. Tel: 212-682-1815
W: www.graphiclabinc.com
Contact person: Chris Campisi
Art on canvas -- Digital Printing – postcards, flyers – Large format posters -- Mounting Laminating, Binding & finishing – Custom projects -- Drum scanning – Digital retouching – Trade show graphics – Vinyl Lettering – Digital C-prints – Digital camera photoprints

Great American Printing
Tel: 800-440-2368.

Original Card Company
Tel: 800-587-2640.
www.originalcards.com

Modern Postcard
Tel: 800-959-8365.
www.modernpostcard.com

Post Script Press
Tel: 800-511-2009.
www.psprint.com

IRIS GICLÉE PRINTING

Omega Fine Art, 9 Tartan Ct., Andover, NJ 07821. Tel: 973-448-7000. Toll free: 888-225-2125. E: omega@warwick.net
Omega provides the highest quality IRIS Giclée Printing & related services to galleries, publishers, and individual artists. Miniature to Grand format on paper & canvas. All archival materials.

PHOTOGRAPHY

Photographics Unlimited
17 West 17 St., New York, NY
10011. Tel: 212-255-9678
Professional photography of 2-D
artwork on the premises. Slides,
photographs, slide dupes, other
services.

Bob Sasson
Tel: 212-675-0973
Photography Specialist for beginner
and established artists. Impressive
results help further your career. Professional quality slides, transparencies, digital, prints. Call for an appointment.

**Jellybean Photographics
and Imaging**
99 Madison Ave., 14th floor, New
York, NY 10016. Tel: 212-679-4888.
All photographic services including
black and white, color and digital.

ADVERTISING AND
GRAPHIC DESIGN

ADS2GO New York, Inc.
The Piano Factory, 454 West 46 St.,
Suite 5ES, New York, NY 10036
Tel: 212-333-3357/914-633-6671
E: denapoliart@optonline.net
W: www.ads2gony.com
A full-service advertising agency.
Ads, direct pieces, collateral, bro-
chures, promo, logo design, videos,
website design, signage, packaging,
corporate identity, concepting. Small
and large clients welcome.

**Artigiana Graphic Design
Andrea Gengo**
118-21 Queens Blvd., Suite 502,
Forest Hills, NY 11375
Tel: 718-261-1445
E: andrea@agd-studio.com
W: artigianagraphicdesign.com

Specializing in identity packages and
sales materials of any scope.
Printed pieces, web design, promotional items communicating your
goals and ideas. Reasonable rates.
Call for an appointment.

Marcy Gold: Art of Gold
30 River Ct., Apt 2405, Jersey City,
NJ 07310-2110. Tel: 201-626-5771
E: Goldbrush3@aol.com
W: MarcyGold.com
Graphic design services for fine
artists. Logos, business cards, let-
terheads, brochures to tastefully
showcase your art. Reasonable
rates.

Mildred Kaye
87 Kern Pl., Saddle Brook, NJ 07663
Tel: 201-843-7651.
E: millyK@artniks.com
W: artniks.com/digitalservices
Quality scans, on CD-ROMs, mod-
erately priced, your image on the
label. Also, designing and formatting
of promotional pieces. 8" x 10" prints
of your images.

MAILING LISTS

Caroll Michels
200 Cocoanut Avenue, #2, Sarasota,
FL 34236
E: carollmich@aol.com
W: www.carollmichels.com
Arts-related mailing lists including
museums and independent curators;
art consultants; New York City critics; international, national and regional arts press; and New York City
arts press.

WEBSITE DESIGN / HOSTING

Clearweave Corporation
219 South Main St., Ste. 203, Ann
Arbor, MI 48104. T: 800-886-9545
Email: info@clearweave.com
Contact person: Colin O'Brien

Beautiful and easy-to-update web sites for artists & small businesses. New (and renewed) sites designed by artists to meet your needs. Photo and text preparation, domain names and hosting.

CAREER GUIDANCE

Art Information Center
55 Mercer St., New York, NY 10012. T: 212-966-3443.
Dan Concholar, Director, counsels artists about NYC galleries and offers direction on appropriate galleries for their work.

Artist Resource Kollectiv
T: 718-745-2366.
E: arkinc@nyc.rr.com
Consultants specializing in developing marketing plans, promotional strategies and presentation tools for artists, art groups and galleries.

Frank Bruno
710 Collegeville Rd., Collegeville, PA 19426. T: 610-489-4213
E: frank-bruno@comcast.net
W: www.artistfrankbruno.com
Art marketing and career coaching: This professional artist offers experienced career advice to beginning and emerging artists. Creating strong support materials, approaching galleries, target marketing and much more included.

Renée Phillips
200 East 72 St., New York, NY 10021. T: 212-472-1660
E: Renee@ManhattanArts.com
W: www.ManhattanArts.com
24 years experience as a career consultant and coach for artists and agents of all career levels, styles and media. Marketing and networking leads, promotional strategies and writing and editing services. Private consultations and group workshops.

THERAPY

Sandra Indig, C.S.W., A.T.R.-B.C.
T: 212-330-6787
An artist, arts therapist and analytic psychotherapist. To experience full expression of one's talent is a primary goal.

WRITING SERVICES

Ed McCormack
217 East 85 St., PMB 228, New York, NY 10028. T: 212-861-0683
E: galleryandstudio@mindspring.com
New York writer and critic available for catalogue essays for artists, galleries and museums.

FINE ART CUSTOM FRAMING

Jadite Galleries
Andres Betancourt
662 10th Avenue (between 46 and 47 St.), New York, NY 10036
T: 212-977-6190
E: JADITEART@aol.com
W: JADITEART.com
Conservation quality picture framing, selected frames and mats, acid free materials, shadow boxes, float and dry mounting, canvas stretching. Original art and posters for sale. Discount to artists. Free delivery.

Julio Valdez Studio
176 East 106th St., 4th Fl, New York, NY 10029. T: 212-426-6260
E: silkaquatint@hotmail.com
W: www.latinamericamaster.com
Fine art, archival quality custom framing at affordable prices. Serving artists, galleries and institutions. Free pick up and delivery in Manhattan with order of $300. or more. Wide range of styles. Fast turnaround.

ART TOURS

Alfred Pommer "New York City Cultural Walking Tours"
285 Avenue C, Apt# 6F, New York, NY 10009
T: 212-979-2388
E: pommerwalk@rcn.com
W: www.nycwalk.com
26 tours focusing on history and architecture. Publicly scheduled and private tours by Alfred Pommer licensed New York guide, college graduate, native New Yorker.

FOUNDRIES

New York ArtCrave Foundry
Tel/Fax: 646-827-9317
W: www.artcrave.com
They cast originals and will custom produce almost any bronze from a photo or artist's drawing. They do metal alloys-compounds casting, moldmaking, and more.

Johnson Atelier
60 Ward Avenue Extension, Mercerville, NJ 08619.
Tel: 609-890-7777

Modern Art Foundry
1870 41st Street, Long Island City, NY 11105
Tel: 718-728-2030

ART STORAGE

Filebank, Inc.
28 Courtland St., S Paterson, NJ 07503
T: 800-625-7163 or 973-279-4411
E: filebankinc@filebankinc.com
W: www.filebankinc.com
Located 20 minutes outside New York City, Filebank provides highly secure, climate controlled vault storage for artwork. They offer an online photographic inventory to their clients.

Index

Please visit

MANHATTAN ARTS
INTERNATIONAL

www.ManhattanArts.com

New, Expanded & Revised Third Edition

PRESENTATION POWER TOOLS FOR FINE ARTISTS

This book is the perfect cure for any visual artist who has ever suffered from writer's block.

Renée Phillips and other experts in the field of art marketing and art promotion offer simple, step-by-step writing guidelines to help you create polished, professional written documents.

Many actual samples of business letters, résumés, biographies, exhibition and grant proposals, gallery contracts, promotional materials, press releases, and artist's statements are provided.

You can follow the formats that are available and tailor them to fit all of your professional needs.

Praise for the Book

"The guidelines are concise and clear. This book provides the artist with the tools to take control of their career. It is a must read for professionals and students." **Diane Leon, Artist and Adjunct Assistant Professor of Arts, New York University**

"A must for every art individual who wants to present themselves professionally." **Linda Handler, Artist and Director, Phoenix Gallery, New York, NY**

"This book helps art professionals organize and simplify their lives." Many effective tools are provided to empower them and tremendously benefit their portfolios." **Susan Schear, Director, Artist Career Planning Services**

To order use the order form on page 235 or go to www.ManhattanArts.com or call 212-472-1660

The Complete Guide To
NEW YORK ART GALLERIES
The Only Comprehensive Resource Of Its Kind

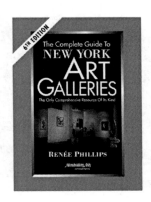

More than 1,000 Detailed Profiles
- Commercial Galleries
- Private Dealers • Non-Profit Venues
- Alternative Spaces • Cultural Centers
- Corporate Art Buyers • Museums
- Artists' Organizations • NYC Artists'
Studios • NYC Artists' Web sites

What You'll Find
- Owner/Director Names • Address • Telephone • Fax • E-mail
- Web site • Owner's Background • Year Established • Work
Shown • 5 Artists & Description of their Work • Gallery's Focus
- Number of Annual Exhibitions • Advertising Venues • Price Range
- Primary Markets • How/When They Select Their Artists
- How/When Artists Should Approach Them • What Materials are
Required / Response Time • Exhibition fees, if any • More!

Praise for the Book
"The only comprehensive resource of its kind. It is invaluable to any artist seeking to gain access to New York galleries. This book helps artists to better market their work." **Matthew Deleget, New York Foundation for the Arts**

"No journal better serves the aspiring artist or tourist." **Ivan Karp, O.K. Harris Works of Art**

"An invaluable resource for art professionals who are seeking a shoe-in to the art world." **Jill O'Connor, art critic, writer for *Sculpture*, *Contemporary*, and *New York Arts***

To order use the order form on page 235 or go to www.ManhattanArts.com or call 212-472-1660

The book is also sold at Barnes & Noble, Museum of Modern Art, O.K. Harris Gallery, A.I Friedman Art Supplies and other stores.

Book Buyers and Arts Organizations

If you would like to order several copies of this book or any of our books for members of your organization, students in your class, artists in your gallery or visitors to your art supply or book store please contact Bert Geller, Book Dept.

Please inquire about our quantity discounts.

MANHATTAN ARTS
INTERNATIONAL

200 East 72 Street, Suite 26L

New York, NY 10021

212-472-1660

Bert@ManhattanArts.com

www.ManhattanArts.com

ORDER FORM

Name _____

Address _____

City _____

State _____ Zip _____

Tel: _____ Email: _____

# of copies	Item	Cost	Total
____	Success Now! For Artists	$25	_____
____	The Complete Guide to New York Art Galleries	$29	_____
____	Presentation Power Tools For Fine Artists	$25	_____
	All three books to one address.............................$75		_____
		TOTAL	_____

- Book and subscription orders available to U.S. residents only.
- Rates include NY State tax, shipping and handling.
- Rush charge available. Please inquire.

If paying by check or money order please make payable to Manhattan Arts International, 200 East 72 Street, Suite 26-L, New York, NY 10021. Tel: 212-472-1660.   E-mail: info@ManhattanArts.com

Name as it appears on the credit card:

_____

___MC ___VISA ___Expiration date _____

Card # _____

Signature _____

Thank you for your order!

MANHATTAN ARTS
INTERNATIONAL

RENÉE PHILLIPS

Artist Advocate
Public Speaker
Career Consultant

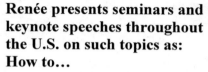

**Renée presents seminars and
keynote speeches throughout
the U.S. on such topics as:
How to...**

- Sell Your Art
- Break into New York Art Galleries
- Raise The Volume on Self-Promotion
- Achieve Your Career Goals
- Create Powerful Presentation Materials
- Turn Your Passion into Profit

She has appeared at:

Barnes & Noble
Katonah Museum
Columbia University
New York University
Artists Talk on Art
Women's Studio Center
City College
The Silvermine Guild
New York Artists Equity Association
American Museum of the Moving Image
American Society of Contemporary Artists
and many other art and educational institutions.

International Art Expo New York
Heckscher Museum
Flushing Arts Council
The Salmagundi Club
Chicago Artists Coalition
Salute to Women in the Arts
Marymount Manhattan College
New York Foundation for the Arts

To arrange for Renée Phillips to present a seminar
please contact Michael Jason: 212-472-1660 or
MJ@ManhattanArts.com

For a current schedule of Renée's seminars
please contact Alexandra Shaw at 212-472-1660 or go to
www.ManhattanArts.com

Renée Phillips is seeking Artists
To feature in her books

Renée is seeking creative individuals who embody the true spirit of the Artrepreneur. They will be featured in her upcoming books.

How have dared to take a risk? Moved out of your comfort zone? Pushed the edge? Turned a tragedy into triumph? Defeated the odds? Stepped outside the box?

How have you made a difference in your career, your community, or the world at large?

Whether it was a single event or a major life change Renée Phillips, The Artrepreneur Coach and motivational speaker, wants to know how.

Please send a description in 100 words or less and your name and contact information to Renee@manhattanarts.com. (No attachments please.)

You will receive a response from us with additional inquiries.

For more information visit www.ManhattanArts.com

About the Author
RENÉE PHILLIPS

Renée Phillips is the author of two editions of *Success Now! For Artists: A Motivational Guide For The Artrepreneur,* three editions of *Presentation Power Tools For Fine Artists,* and six editions of *The Complete Guide To New York Art Galleries,* the only comprehensive resource of its kind. She is founder and Editor-in-Chief of *Manhattan Arts International* magazine, now online at www.ManhattanArts.com. She is Editor-in-Chief of *The Artrepreneur Newsletter.*

As founder and director of Manhattan Arts International, she is dedicated to building relationships among members of the art community and art enthusiasts. She is a pioneer in her field as a career advisor and coach to artists and agents, helping her clients reach their potential.

Renée's motivational seminars and keynote speeches have been held at many universities and art venues including International Art Expo NY, American Museum of the Moving Image, Columbia University, and New York Foundation for the Arts. She presents "How to Sell Your Art" at The Learning Annex in New York, NY. As a faculty member of Marymount Manhattan College she conducted gallery and studio tours and presented a series of Artist and Business seminars.

As an artist's advocate Renée has been awarded citations from two NYC mayors. She was featured in *New York Newsday* as a "Community Leader." Articles about her have appeared in *The New York Times, Crain's New York Business,* and *Our Town.*

Her articles have been published by numerous publications including *The Artist's Proof,* a publication of New York Artists Equity Association, an artist advocacy organization, in which she held a position on the Board of Directors. Renée is currently Vice-President of Artists Advocacy of the Women's Studio Center and a member of ARTTABLE and the International Association of Art Critics.

She has juried and curated numerous multi-media art exhibitions in art and alternative venues including Lincoln Center and First Women's Bank, many of which received national TV and international print coverage. She organized the "*Manhattan Arts* Debate," the only political debate in NYC's history to concentrate solely on the arts.

Renée studied art at the Art Students League in New York, NY. As a professional artist she had many solo and group exhibitions. Although she is no longer a practicing artist her work is in many private and public collections including Merrill Lynch and Chase Manhattan Bank.